EURIPIDES · II

The Cyclops
Heracles
Iphigenia in Tauris
Helen

THE COMPLETE GREEK TRAGEDIES

Edited by David Grene and Richmond Lattimore

EURIPIDES · II

THE CYCLOPS

Translated by William Arrowsmith

HERACLES

Translated by William Arrowsmith

IPHIGENIA IN TAURIS

Translated by Witter Bynner

HELEN

Translated by Richmond Lattimore

THE UNIVERSITY OF CHICAGO PRESS

CHICAGO & LONDON

THE UNIVERSITY OF CHICAGO PRESS, CHICAGO 60637
The University of Chicago Press, Ltd., London

Published 1956. Paperback Edition 1969
Printed in the United States of America

01 00 99 98 97 96 95 94 93 92   17 18 19 20 21

International Standard Book Number:
0-226-30781-6 (paperbound)
Library of Congress Catalog Card Number: 56-6639

TABLE OF CONTENTS

THE CYCLOPS

Translated by William Arrowsmith

INTRODUCTION TO *CYCLOPS**

INTEREST in Euripides' *Cyclops* is generally justified historically: other than a chunk of Sophocles' *Ichneutae*, it is the only example of a satyr-play, that ribald piece which in the dramatic festivals crowned a group of three tragedies or a tragic trilogy. But the *Cyclops* is more than historically interesting; it is, by modern standards, good fast farce, clearly stageworthy, with a fine dramatic intelligence behind it. The movement is typically Euripidean, not merely in the sharp reversal of roles and sympathies, the crisp dialogue and the consistent anachronization, but in formal structure and underlying idea as well. Moreover, despite the play's sportive obscenity and knockabout humor, its underlying idea is essentially serious. The *Cyclops*, that is, may be clearly a farce, but it is primarily a farce of ideas, a gay and ironic flirtation with the problem of civilized brutality. As such, it lies within the main stream of Euripides' tragic thought, and, if its treatment and tone differ from that of tragedy, the difference is less a difference of dramatic quality or genius than a difference of genre.

We should like to know a great deal more about satyr-drama as a genre than we do, and we should especially like to know what in fifth-century practice was the formal connection between a satyr-play and the three tragedies which preceded it. But unfortunately the *Cyclops* is undated and cannot, with any degree of certainty, be assigned to one of the extant tragedies.[1] In the absence of that crucial

* This play first appeared in the *Hudson Review* (Spring, 1952), Vol. I, No. 1, and is reprinted here by permission.

1. The most tempting suggestion has been, I think, that the *Cyclops* should be assigned to a group of three tragedies of which the extant *Hecuba* was one. (The *Hecuba* is dated, on very good grounds, almost certainly to 425 B.C.) The assignment is strengthened not merely by topical considerations (cf. E. Delebecque, *Euripide et la guerre du Péloponnèse*) but by very close formal resemblances between the two plays. Thus the blinding of Polyphemus parallels the blinding of Polymnestor, and Polyphemus' final appearance from the cave vividly recalls Polymnestor's emergence from the tent. In both plays again, the guiding idea is that of civilized brutality, and in both cases a barbaric vengeance is taken upon a barbarian (Polymnestor,

information, it becomes difficult to speak with assurance of the formal nature of the play or to generalize from it to the formal definition of fifth-century satyr-drama. Indeed, even if we possessed the requisite information, the very distance which separates the tragedy of Euripides from that of Aeschylus and Sophocles would tend by analogy to preclude a generalization about satyr-plays. One ancient writer, it is true, speaks of satyr-drama as being "tragedy-at-play" or "joking tragedy."[2] But this is hardly helpful, since it may mean either that satyr-drama was mock tragedy, or tragedy *buffa*, or pure farce, or simply a sportive treatment of the subject matter of tragedy. All of these are possibilities applicable to the *Cyclops*, but we have no evidence which might allow us to decide among them.

In point of origins the satyr-play, like both comedy and tragedy, was closely bound up with Dionysiac fertility ritual. Even in the fifth century satyr-drama in its frequent obscenity, its conventional use of Silenus as "nurse" and companion of Dionysus, and its chorus of satyrs with their *phalloi* preserves more vividly than tragedy the memory of its origins. What the original connection between tragedy and comedy and "satyr" may have been, we do not know, though Aristotle in a much disputed passage asserts that the satyr-play was one of the early stages of tragedy;[3] but the value of the testimony appears doubtful.[4] On the whole, scholars have preferred to believe that both satyr-drama and tragedy are independent developments of Dionysiac ritual and that satyr-drama was probably adopted by the dramatist Pratinas from a Peloponnesian source and attached to the Attic festivals. Alternatively, it is held that the double aspect of Dionysiac ritual—the mourning for the dead god and the

---

Polyphemus) by a "civilized" person (Hecuba, Odysseus). The final prophecies again closely parallel each other, and the portrayal of Odysseus in the *Hecuba* is given a great deal of point if we have in mind the sequel in *Cyclops*. In the dovetailing of actions and the reversal of roles, the two plays are strikingly similar.

2. Demetrius of Phalerum *De interp.* 169; cf. Horace *Ars poetica* 231–33.

3. *Poetics* 1449ª 9 ff.

4. Cf. A. W. Pickard-Cambridge, *Dithyramb, Tragedy and Comedy* (Oxford, 1927), p. 124.

joyous celebration at his resurrection—accounts for the connection between tragedy and the satyr-play. On this theory tragedy contains the *agon* of the dying god, while the satyr-play, like comedy, exhibits the happy celebration for the reborn god and the ritual of the sacred marriage and rounds off the complete drama of the rite in a sportive coda. The presence in the *Cyclops* of an attenuated *komos* and a hinted mock (male) marriage between Silenus and Polyphemus offers some slight evidence for the theory. But it is this very attenuation of the ritual element in the play that reminds us that a theory of formal origins does not really explain what we need to know—the *literary* use and the meaning of the developed form. An account of origins may perhaps explain the conventions of a given form, but it will seldom explain the conscious literary deployment of those conventions.

For the rest our information is tantalizingly slight. Thus we know that the satyr-plays were briefer than the tragedies (the *Cyclops* is the shortest of extant plays); they had their own peculiar choral dance, the *sikinnis*, and they allowed, in prosody and diction, a very slight relaxation from tragic standards in the direction of colloquial speech. For its material satyr-drama drew upon the same sources in myth and *epos* as tragedy. Thus the *Oresteia* appears to have been followed by the *Proteus*, a satyr-play dealing with Menelaus' Egyptian adventure with the Old Man of the Sea, while the *Cyclops* is a conflation of the Polyphemus episode from the ninth book of the Odyssey with the story of the capture of Dionysus by Lydian pirates.[5] Both the chorus of satyrs and its "father" Silenus form a standard part of satyric convention, and their characters are accordingly stylized: the satyrs are boisterous, childlike "horse-men" (*not* "goat-men") with a strong streak of cowardice, while Silenus is at every point the ancestor of Falstaff—lewd, fat, bald, drunken, boastful, knavish, and foolish. Finally, it needs to be stressed that, however comic a satyr-play may seem, it is not to be confounded with Greek comedy, which differs from it not only in its material (usually free invention or mythological burlesque), but in structure, conventions, and the degree of topicality and license.

5. Cf. *Homeric Hymn to Dionysus.*

In plot and detail Euripides' adaptation of his Homeric material is remarkably close. If Odysseus here does not escape from the cave by clinging to a ram's belly, and if the immense boulder which in Homer blocked the cave has here been rolled away, these are clearly alterations demanded by the necessities of theatrical presentation. In Euripides the Cyclops is still the creature of his belly, a barking barbarian, and Odysseus is still in some sense the shrewd and civilized man who manages by exercise of mother wit to mutilate the man-eating monster and escape. Or so, at least, it might seem if we possessed only the first half of the play. But the *Cyclops* is not merely a dramatic retelling of Homer; rather, it is Homer's parable of the civilized man and the savage systematically anachronized into its fifth-century equivalent, an altogether different parable.

Neither Odysseus nor Polyphemus is really Homeric at all. Odysseus is not the type of the civilized man, and the Euripidean Cyclops, like the United States in Wilde's epigram, has passed directly from barbarism to decadence without pause for civilization. Both manifest late fifth-century types of corruption: Odysseus' Homeric heroism in its new context is systematically undercut, less heroism than a transparent vainglory and depraved eloquence; Polyphemus is less Caliban than Callicles, an outright exponent of philosophical egoism and the immoralist equation of might and right. Euripides has taken considerable pains, moreover, to indicate to his audience that this is no longer Homer's world, but their own. Thus, when Odysseus first appears, he is greeted by Silenus as a "glib sharper" and "son of Sisyphus." Now, whatever Odysseus may be in Homer, he is never merely a "glib sharper," and his father is Laertes, not Sisyphus. To an audience bred on Homer the distinction is revealing: at one blow Euripides deprives Odysseus of his Homeric paternity in order to attach him to Sisyphus, the proverbial type of cheat and thief, and thereby warns his audience of what they may expect. Odysseus is in fact the familiar depraved politician of the *Hecuba*, the *Trojan Women,* and the *Iphigeneia at Aulis;* he stands, as he almost always does in tragedy, for that refinement of intellect and eloquence which makes civilized brutality so much more terrible than mere savagery. In the *Cyclops*, however, he is on the defensive, and there is irony in the reversal of roles as the man who refused mercy and *nomos* to Hecuba must now himself plead for it. If we sympathize with Odysseus at first, this initial sympathy is nonetheless quickly alienated by the sheer, otiose brutality of his revenge and by Polyphemus' transformation into a drunken, almost lovable, buffoon. The gory description of the Cyclops' cannibalism may perhaps justify Odysseus' revenge, but it does not thereby redeem its barbaric cruelty. Just as the full action of the *Hecuba* consists in reducing both Hecuba and the barbarian Polymnestor to a common subhuman cruelty, so the *Cyclops* shows, not the distinction, but the identity, between Odysseus and Polyphemus.

Odysseus' speech for *nomos* and mercy is the crux of the play. As Silenus recognizes, the speech is pure sophistry, but the sophistry has important consequences that we need to examine. The difficulty lies in the thoroughness of the anachronization and the allusions to the sanctions and background of the Peloponnesian War.

It opens with a disclaimer of responsibility for the Trojan War: "A god was responsible; don't blame men." Such disclaimers in Euripides normally operate to damn those who make them, as, for instance, Helen's disavowal of responsibility in the *Trojan Women*. The next argument sounds very strange indeed. The Greeks, Odysseus argues, have preserved the temples of Poseidon (father of Cyclops) and saved Hellas; therefore the Cyclops, who is Greek because he lives in Greek Sicily (another anachronism), should spare Odysseus and his men. What we have here is a covert but unmistakable allusion to the Persian Wars, when Athens claimed to have saved Hellas and the ancestral gods from the Persians. There is irony in the claim that it was piety which saved the silver-mines of Laurium on Cape Sunium (where there happened to be a shrine to Poseidon), but the larger irony is somewhat more complex.

What Odysseus is urging here is nothing more or less than the argument which Athens had used to acquire her empire: Athens had saved Hellas and should have the rewards of her deed. This sanction for empire was employed down to the time of the Peloponnesian War to coerce neutrals and unwilling states into the Athenian orbit, and the sanction was as loathsome to most Greeks as the Athenian

Empire. Herodotus, writing in the forties, is so much aware of the unpopularity of Athens and her sanction that he is reluctant to state the real truth which underlies the sanction—Athens *did* save Hellas. In 432 B.C., just before the outbreak of the Peloponnesian War, the unofficial Athenian envoys at Sparta could say of their empire:

> We have a fair claim to our possessions. . . . We need not refer to remote antiquity . . . but to the Persian War and contemporary history we must refer, although we are rather tired of continually bringing this subject forward.[6]

By 416, the Athenian generals at Melos could argue naked imperialism; the empire had outgrown its sanction:

> We shall not trouble you with specious pretences . . . either of how we have a right to our empire because we overthrew the Persians, or are now attacking you because of wrong that you have done us . . . since you know as well as we do that right, as the world goes, is only in question between equals in power, while the strong do what they can and the weak suffer what they must.[7]

This, then, is the sanction Odysseus urges, and it is one whose irony it would be difficult for his audience to miss. The irony lies in the fact that an argument normally used to deny mercy to others is here being used to obtain it. When it fails before the Cyclops' massive egoism, Odysseus resorts to the ultimate argument of the weak, law and civilized custom (*nomos*). In so doing he joins Thucydides' Plataeans and Melians, as well as his own victim Hecuba. And, like Hecuba, failing to receive *nomos*, he finally resorts to a revenge utterly unsanctioned by any civilized standards, *anomos*. The speech closes on an overt reference to the cost of human suffering in the Peloponnesian War. And here, as so often in Euripides, the really serious argument is put in the mouth of a man who is not qualified to make it, or who contradicts it in his actions. The contradiction lies in the inverted use of the imperialistic sanction and the implied indifference to human suffering in other circumstances.

If Odysseus speaks in part the language of the Athenian im-

6. Thuc. i. 73. 2 ff.

7. *Ibid.* v. 89.

perialists and in part the language of the Melians, the Cyclops outdistances him by far. Devoid of respect for the gods, his religion is his belly and his right his desires. He speaks exactly the language of Plato's Thrasymachus and Callicles, a straightforward egoism resting on an appeal to Nature for the disregard of morality. *Nomos*, so far as he is concerned, is a mere convention of the weak to elude the strong. In the contrast, then, of Polyphemus and Odysseus we have no Homeric contrast of barbarism and cool, civilized intelligence, but a juxtaposition of two related types of civilized brutality whose difference is merely that of circumstance, one being weak, the other strong. It is because neither Cyclops nor Odysseus has any genuine moral dignity, because both of them are shown as effectively brutal and corrupt, that the bloody blinding of Polyphemus can come as close to pathos as it does without becoming any less comic.

The ending is in fact superbly controlled. As usual in Euripides, the sympathy invoked for one character is suddenly alienated and shifted to another; the victim and the oppressor change places. Polyphemus, from being first a Homeric cannibal and then a Euripidean Callicles, is suddenly turned into a decadent, rather likable buffoon who loathes war, understands generosity, and tipsily "rapes" Silenus. Odysseus makes his bid for glory by blinding this cannibal oaf while he sleeps drunkenly. The shift in sympathy is not decisive, because no real principle is involved; but it is not therefore illusory. Odysseus' action is contemptible, but not quite criminal; Polyphemus gets what he deserves, but we pity him. That we are meant to view the action in this way seems clear both in Polyphemus' final prophecy of trouble for Odysseus and in Odysseus' statement that he would have done wrong had he burned Troy but not avenged his men. Whatever his rights in avenging his men may be, they are not sanctioned by the burning of Troy, an action which the Cyclops condemns, and with him Euripides. The truth is that Odysseus and the Cyclops deserve, not justice, but each other. The *Cyclops* in its seriousness and its humor plays about a struggle for justice between two men who either distort justice or deny its existence and who cannot therefore meaningfully claim it when wronged. And yet they get it.

THE CYCLOPS

CHARACTERS

Silenus

Chorus of satyrs

Coryphaeus, or chorus-leader

Odysseus

Cyclops, called Polyphemus

Members of Odysseus' crew

Slaves

THE CYCLOPS

SCENE: *An enormous cave at the foot of Mt. Etna. In the foreground, a slope of pasture; on the right, a small brook. Silenus comes out of the cave to speak the prologue. He is old, fat, and bald. A horse's tail hangs down his legs. He wears a filthy tunic and carries a rake.*

Silenus

O Bromios,
thanks to you, my troubles are as many now
as in my youth when my body still was strong!
First I remember when Hera drove you mad
and you left your nurses, the mountain nymphs.
And then there was that war with the Giants:
there I stood, on your right, covering your flank
with my spear. And I hit Enceladus
square on the button of his shield and killed him.
Or wait: was that in a dream? No, by Zeus,
for I showed the very spoils to Bacchus.
And now I must bail against a wilder wave
of trouble. For when I heard that Hera
had pricked on those Lydian pirates to sell you
as a slave abroad, I hoisted sail with my sons
to search for you. Right on the stern I stood,
the tiller in my hands, steering the ship.
And my boys strained at the oars, churning white
the green sea in our search for you, my king!
And then we had almost made Malea
when an east wind cracked down and drove us here,
to rocky Etna, where the one-eyed sons
of the sea-god, the murderous Cyclopes,
live in their desolate caves. One of them—
they call him Polyphemus—captured us
and made us slaves in his house. So now,
instead of dancing in the feasts of Bacchus,

we herd the flocks of this godless Cyclops.
Down at the foot of the mountain, my sons—
young men all of them—watch the youngling herd.
I am assigned to stay and fill the troughs
and clean the quarters and play the chef
for the loathsome dinners of the Cyclops.
And now I must scour the cave with this rake—
these are my orders—to welcome back home
my absent master and his flock of sheep.

(He halts suddenly, turns to the left and looks. A confused hubbub, mingled with singing, offstage.)

But I see my sons shepherding their sheep
this way. What? (*Shouts.*) How can you dance like that?
Do you think you're mustered at Bacchus' feast
and mincing your lewd way with lyre-music
to the halls of Althaea?

(Preceded by a flute-player and driving their herds before them, the chorus of satyrs bounds into the orchestra. Except for short goat-skin jerkins, they are naked. About their waists they wear belts—skin-colored—to each of which is fixed, in front, a phallus, and in the rear, a horse's tail. They do a series of fast and intricate steps as they push the stubborn rams, coax the ewes, and round up the strays.)

Chorus

(To a ewe who dashes for the slope.)

STROPHE

You there, with the fine pedigree
on both sides, dam and sire,
  why run for the rocks?
Haven't you here a quiet breeze,
  green grass for the grazing?
Look: the water from the brook
  beside the cave
  swirls through your troughs
  and the small lambs bleat.

(*To an obstinate ram.*)

Hey, you too? Are you off as well
to crop on the dew on the hill?
Move, or I'll pelt you with stones!
In with you, horny-head, move along
into the fold of Shepherd Cyclops!

(*To a stubborn ewe.*)

ANTISTROPHE

Relieve your swollen teats!
Come, suckle your young whom you left
  all alone in the lamb-pens!
Asleep all day, your new-born lambs
  bleat that they want you.
Leave your cropping and into the fold,
  into the rocks of Etna!

[Hey, you too? Are you off as well
to crop on the dew on the hill?
Move, or I'll pelt you with stones!
In with you, horny-head, move along
into the fold of Shepherd Cyclops!]

EPODE

No Bacchus here! Not here the dance,
or the women whirling the *thyrsos*,
or the timbrels shaken,
where the springs rill up!
Not here the gleam of wine,
and no more at Nysa with nymphs;
crying *Iacchos! Iacchos!*
Where is Aphrodite? . . .
she that I used to fly after
along with the bare-footed Bacchae!
Dear lord Bacchus, where do you run,
tossing your auburn hair?
For I, your servant, am a wretched slave,
tricked out in dirty goatskin

to serve a one-eyed Cyclops,
and out of the way, lord, of your love.

(Silenus, who has been scanning anxiously the horizon on the right, turns suddenly, his finger on his lips.)

Silenus

Be quiet, my sons. Quick, order the slaves
to corral the flocks into the rock-fold.

Coryphaeus

Move along there.

(Slaves appear and hustle the animals into the cave.)

But why this hurry, father?

Silenus

I see a Greek ship drawn up on the shore
and oarsman led by a captain coming
toward our cave. They carry water-pitchers
and empty containers about their necks:
they'll want supplies. Poor strangers, who are they?
They can't know our master Polyphemus,
coming like this to the maneater's cave
and looking for a welcome in his maw.
But hush, so we can learn from where they've come,
and why, to Sicily and Mt. Etna.

(Odysseus appears on the right. He carries a sword. A wine-flask made of skin is suspended from his neck; a cup is attached to the cord. He is followed by crew-members carrying pitchers and jugs.)

Odysseus

Strangers, could you tell us where we might find
running water? We have nothing to drink.
Would some one of you like to sell some food
to hungry sailors? *What?* Do I see right?
We must have come to the city of Bacchus.
These are satyrs I see around the cave.
Let me greet the oldest among you first.

Silenus

Greeting, stranger. Who are you, and from where?

Odysseus

I am Odysseus of Ithaca, king of the Cephallenians.

Silenus

I've heard of you: a glib sharper, Sisyphus' bastard.

Odysseus

I am he. Keep your abuse to yourself.

Silenus

From what port did you set sail for Sicily?

Odysseus

We come from Troy and from the war there.

Silenus

What? Couldn't you chart your passage home?

Odysseus

We were driven here by wind and storm.

Silenus

Too bad. I had the same misfortune.

Odysseus

You too were driven from your course by storm?

Silenus

We were chasing the pirates who captured Bacchus.

Odysseus

What is this place? Is it inhabited?

Silenus

This is Etna, the highest peak in Sicily.

Odysseus

Where are the walls and the city-towers?

Silenus

This is no city. No man inhabits here.

Odysseus
Who does inhabit it? Wild animals?

Silenus
The Cyclopes. They live in caves, not houses.

Odysseus
Who governs them? Or do the people rule?

Silenus
They are savages. There is no government.

Odysseus
How do they live? Do they till the fields?

Silenus
Their whole diet is milk, cheese, and meat.

Odysseus
Do they grow grapes and make the vine give wine?

Silenus
No. The land is sullen. There is no dance.

Odysseus
Are they hospitable to strangers here?

Silenus
Strangers, they say, make excellent eating.

Odysseus
What? You say they feast on human flesh?

Silenus
Here every visitor is devoured.

Odysseus
Where is this Cyclops now? In the . . . house?

Silenus
Gone hunting on Mt. Etna with his packs.

Odysseus
What should we do to make our escape?

Silenus
I don't know, Odysseus. We'll do what we can.

Odysseus
Then sell us some bread. We have none left.

Silenus
There is nothing to eat, I said, except meat.

Odysseus
Meat is good, and it will stop our hunger.

Silenus
We do have fig-cheese. And there is milk.

Odysseus
Bring it out. The buyer should see what he buys.

Silenus
Tell me, how much are you willing to pay?

Odysseus
In money, nothing. But I have some . . . wine.

Silenus
Delicious word! How long since I've heard it.

Odysseus
Maron, son of a god, gave me this wine.

Silenus
Not the same lad I once reared in these arms?

Odysseus
The son of Bacchus himself, to be brief.

Silenus
Where is the wine? on board ship? you have it?

Odysseus
In this flask, old man. Look for yourself.

Silenus
That? That wouldn't make one swallow for me.

Odysseus
No? For each swallow you take, the flask gives two.

Silenus
A fountain among fountains, that! I *like* it.

Odysseus
Will you have it unwatered to start with?

Silenus
That's fair. The buyer should have a sample.

Odysseus
I have a cup here to go with the flask.

Silenus
Pour away. A drink will joggle my memory.

Odysseus
(*Unstoppers the flask, pours out a cup and waves it under Silenus' nose.*)
There you are.

Silenus
Mmmmmm. Gods, what a bouquet!

Odysseus
Can you *see* it?

Silenus
No, by Zeus, but I can whiff it.

Odysseus
Have another. Then you'll *sing* its praises.

Silenus
Mmmmmmaa. A dance for Bacchus! La de da.

Odysseus
Did that purl down your gullet sweetly?

Silenus
Right down to the tips of my toenails.

Odysseus
Besides the wine, we'll give you money.

Silenus
Money be damned! Just pour out the wine.

Odysseus
Then bring out your cheese, or some lambs.

Silenus

Right away.
I don't give a hoot for any master.
I would go mad for one cup of that wine!
I'd give away the herds of all the Cyclopes.
Once I get drunk and happy, I'd go jump
in the sea off the Leucadian rock!
The man who doesn't like to drink is mad.
Why, when you're drunk, you stand up stiff down here

(*Gestures.*)

and then get yourself a fistful of breast
and browse on the soft field ready to your hands.
You dance, and goodbye to troubles. Well then,
why shouldn't I adore a drink like that
and be damned to the stupid Cyclops
with his eye in the middle?

(*He enters the cave.*)

Coryphaeus

Listen, Odysseus, we'd like a word with you.

Odysseus

By all means. We are all friends here.

Coryphaeus

Did you take Helen when you took Troy?

Odysseus

We rooted out the whole race of Priam.

Coryphaeus

When you took that woman, did you all take turns
and bang her? She liked variety in men,
the fickle bitch! Why, the sight of a man
with embroidered pants and a golden chain
so fluttered her, she left Menelaus,
a fine little man. I wish there were
no women in the world—except for me.

(*Silenus reappears from the cave, his arms loaded with wicker panniers of cheese; he leads some lambs.*)

Silenus

King Odysseus, here are some lambs for you,
the fat of the flock, and here, a good stock
of creamed cheeses. Take them and leave the cave
as fast as you can. But first give me a drink
of that blessed wine to seal our bargain.
Help us! Here comes the Cyclops! What shall we do?

Odysseus

We're finished now, old man. Where can we run?

Silenus

Into the cave. You can hide in there.

Odysseus

Are you mad? Run right into the trap?

Silenus

No danger. The rocks are full of hiding-places.

Odysseus

(*Grandiloquently.*)

Never. Why, Troy itself would groan aloud
if we ran from one man. Many's the time
I stood off ten thousand Phrygians with my shield.
If die we must, we must die with honor.
If we live, we live with our old glory!

(*The satyrs run pell-mell around the orchestra; Silenus slinks into the cave. On the left appears a bearded man of great height. He holds a club and is followed by dogs.*)

Cyclops

Here. Here. What's going on? What's this uproar?
Why this Bacchic hubbub? There's no Bacchus here,
no bronze clackers or rattling castanets!
How are my newborn lambs in the cave?
Are they at the teat, nuzzling their mothers?
Are the wicker presses filled with fresh cheese?
Well? What do you say? Answer, or my club
will drub the tears out of you! Look up, not down.

Coryphaeus

There. We're looking right up at Zeus himself.
I can see Orion and all the stars.

Cyclops

Is my dinner cooked and ready to eat?

Coryphaeus

Ready and waiting. You have only to bolt it.

Cyclops

And are the vats filled up, brimming with milk?

Coryphaeus

You can swill a whole hogshead, if you like.

Cyclops

Cow's milk, or sheep's milk, or mixed?

Coryphaeus

Whatever you like. Just don't swallow me.

Cyclops

You least. I'd soon be dead if I had you
jumping through your capers in my belly.

(*He suddenly sees the Greeks standing near the cave.*)

Hey! what's that crowd I see over by the cave?
Have pirates or thieves taken the country?
Look: sheep from my fold tied up with withies!
And cheese-presses all around! And the old man
with his bald head swollen red with bruises!

(*Silenus emerges from the cave, groaning; he is red-faced from the wine.*)

Silenus

Ohhh. I'm all on fire. They've beaten me up.

Cyclops

Who did? Who's been beating your head, old man?

Silenus

(*Indicating the Greeks.*)

They did, Cyclops. I wouldn't let them rob you.

Cyclops

Didn't they know that I am a god?
Didn't they know my ancestors were gods?

Silenus

I tried to tell them. But they went on robbing.
I tried to stop them from stealing your lambs
and eating your cheeses. What's more, they said
they would yoke you to a three-foot collar
and squeeze out your bowels through your one eye,
and scourge your backsides with a whip,
and then they were going to tie you up
and throw you on a ship and give you away
for lifting rocks or for work at a mill.

Cyclops

Is that so? Run and sharpen my cleavers.
Take a big bunch of faggots and light it.
I'll murder them right now and stuff my maw
with their meat hot from the coals. Why wait
to carve? I'm fed up with mountain food:
too many lions and stags and too long
since I've had a good meal of manmeat.

Silenus

And quite right, master. A change in diet
is very pleasant. It's been a long time
since we've had visitors here at the cave.

Odysseus

Cyclops, let your visitors have their say.
We came here to your cave from our ship
because we needed food. This fellow here
sold us some lambs in exchange for wine—
all quite voluntary, no coercion.
There's not a healthy word in what he says;
the fact is he was caught peddling your goods.

Silenus

I? Why, damn your soul.

Odysseus

If I'm lying. . . .

Silenus

I swear, Cyclops, by your father Poseidon,
by Triton the great, I swear by Nereus,
by Calypso and by Nereus' daughters,
by the holy waves and every species of fish,
I swear, dear master, sweet little Cyclops,
I did not sell your goods to the strangers!
If I did, then let my dear children die for it.

Coryphaeus

And the same to you. With these very eyes
I saw you selling goods to the strangers.
And if I'm lying, then let my father
die for it. But don't do wrong to strangers.

Cyclops

You're lying. I would rather believe him

(*He indicates Silenus.*)

than Rhadamanthus himself. And I say
that he's right. But I want to question you.
Where have you come from, strangers? where to?
And tell me in what city you grew up.

Odysseus

We are from Ithaca. After we sacked
the city of Troy, sea-winds drove us here,
safe and sound, to your country, Cyclops.

Cyclops

Was it you who sacked Troy-on-Scamander
because that foul Helen was carried off?

Odysseus

We did. Our terrible task is done.

Cyclops

You ought to die for shame: to go to war
with the Phrygians for a single woman!

Odysseus

A god was responsible; don't blame men.
But we ask as free men, we implore you,
do not, O noble son of the sea-god,
murder men who come to your cave as friends.
Do not profane your mouth by eating us.

(*He waxes rhetorical.*)

For it is we, my lord, who everywhere
in Hellas preserved your father Poseidon
in the tenure of his temples. Thanks to us,
Taenarus' sacred harbor is inviolate;
the peak of Sunium with its silver-lodes
sacred to Athena, is still untouched;
and safe, the sanctuaries of Geraestus!
We did not betray Greece—perish the thought!—
to Phrygians. And you have a share in this:
for this whole land, under volcanic Etna
in whose depths you live, is part of Hellas.

(*The Cyclops shows disapproval.*)

In any case—and if you disagree—
all men honor that custom whereby
shipwrecked sailors are clothed and protected.
Above all, they should not gorge your mouth and paunch,
nor be spitted as men might spit an ox.
The land of Priam has exhausted Greece,
soaked up the blood of thousands killed in war:
wives made widows, women without their sons,
old men turned snow-white. If you roast the rest
for your ungodly meal, where will Hellas turn?
Change your mind, Cyclops! Forget your hunger!
Forget this sacrilege and do what is right.
Many have paid the price for base profits.

Silenus

A word of advice, Cyclops. If you eat
all of his flesh and chew on his tongue,
you'll become eloquent and very glib.

Cyclops

Money's the wise man's religion, little man.
The rest is mere bluff and purple patches.
I don't give a damn for my father's shrines
along the coast! Why did you think I would?
And I'm not afraid of Zeus's thunder;
in fact, I don't believe Zeus is stronger
than I am. And anyway I don't care,
and I'll tell you why I don't care. When Zeus
pours down rain, I take shelter in this cave
and feast myself on roast lamb or venison.
Then I stretch myself and wash down the meal,
flooding my belly with a vat of milk.
Then, louder than ever Zeus can thunder,
I fart through the blankets. When the wind sweeps down
with snow from Thrace, I wrap myself in furs
and light up the fire. Then let it snow
for all I care! Whether it wants or not,
the earth must grow the grass that feeds my flocks.
And as for sacrifices, I make mine,
not to the gods, but the greatest god of all,
this belly of mine! To eat, to drink
from day to day, to have no worries—
that's the real Zeus for your clever man!
As for those who embroider human life
with their little laws—damn the lot of them!
I shall go right on indulging myself—
by eating you. But, to be in the clear,
I'll be hospitable and give you fire
and my father's water—plus a cauldron.
Once it starts to boil, it will render down
your flesh very nicely. So, inside with you,
and gather round the altar to the god
of the cave, and wish him hearty eating.

(*Cyclops enters the cave, driving Odysseus' crew before him.*)

Odysseus

Gods! Have I escaped our hardships at Troy
and on the seas only to be cast up
and wrecked on the reef of this savage heart?
O Pallas, lady, daughter of Zeus, now
if ever, help me! Worse than war at Troy,
I have come to my danger's deepest place.
O Zeus, god of strangers, look down on me
from where you sit, throned among the bright stars!
If you do not look down upon me now,
you are no Zeus, but a nothing at all!

(*He disappears into the cave; Silenus follows him.*)

Chorus

Open the vast O of your jaws, Cyclops!
Dinner is served: the limbs of your guests,
boiled, roasted, or broiled, ready for you
  to gnaw, rend, and chew
while you loll on your shaggy goatskin.

Don't ask me to dinner. Stow that cargo
on your own. Let me keep clear of this cave,
well clear of the Cyclops of Etna,
  this loathsome glutton,
who gorges himself on the guts of his guests!

Savage! Stranger to mercy! A monster
who butchers his guests on his hearth,
who boils up their flesh and bolts it,
  whose foul mouth munches
on human meat plucked from the sizzling coals!

(*Odysseus appears from the cave.*)

Odysseus

Zeus, how can I say what I saw in that cave?
Unbelievable horrors, the kind of things
men do in myths and plays, not in real life!

Coryphaeus

Has that god-forsaken Cyclops butchered
your crew? Tell us what happened, Odysseus.

Odysseus

He snatched up two of my men, the soundest
and heaviest. He weighed them in his hands.

Coryphaeus

How horrible! How could you stand to watch?

Odysseus

First, after we had entered the cave,
he lit a fire and tossed down on the huge hearth
logs from a vast oak—you would have needed
three wagons merely to carry the load.
Then he pulled his pallet of pine-needles
close to the fire. After he milked the sheep,
he filled a hundred-gallon vat with milk.
By his side, he put an ivy-wood box,
nearly four feet in width and six feet deep.
Next he put a cauldron of brass to boil
on the fire, and beside it thorn-wood spits
whose points had been sharpened in the coals
and the rest trimmed down with an axe. There were
bowls for catching blood, big as Etna,
and set flush against the blade of the axe.
Well, when this damned cook of Hades was ready,
he snatched up two of my men. With one blow
he slit the throat of one over the lip
of the brass cauldron. Holding the other
by the heels, he slammed him against a rock
and bashed out his brains. Then he hacked away
the flesh with his terrible cleaver
and put the pieces to roast on the coals.
The leftovers he tossed in the pot to boil.
With the tears streaming down, I went up close
and waited on the Cyclops. The others,

their faces ashen, huddled up like birds
in the crannies of the rocks. Then he leaned back,
bloated with his awful meal on my men,
and let out a staggering belch. Just then
some god sent me a marvelous idea!
I filled a cup and gave him Maron's wine
to drink. "Cyclops," I said, "son of the sea-god,
see what a heavenly drink yield the grapes
of Greece, the gladness of Dionysus!"
Glutted with his dreadful meal, he took it
and drained it off at one gulp, then lifted
his hands in thanks: "You are the best of guests!
You have given me a noble drink to crown
a noble meal." When I saw how pleased he was,
I poured him another, knowing the wine
would quickly fuddle him and pay him back.
Then he started to sing. I poured one drink
after another and warmed his belly.
So there he is, inside, singing away
while my crew wails; you can hear the uproar.
I slipped quietly out. Now, if you agree,
I'd like to save myself and you as well.
So tell me, yes or no, whether you want
to escape this monster and live with the nymphs
in the halls of Bacchus. Your father in there
agrees, but he's weak and loves his liquor.
He's stuck to the cup as though it were glue,
and can't fly. But you are young, so follow me
and save yourselves; find again your old friend,
Dionysus, so different from this Cyclops!

Coryphaeus

My good friend, if only we might see that day
when we escape at last this godless Cyclops!

(*Showing his phallus.*)

This poor hose has been a bachelor
a long time now. But we can't eat the Cyclops *back!*

Odysseus

Listen to my plan for setting you free
and our revenge upon this loathsome beast.

Coryphaeus

Tell on. I would rather hear tell of his death
than hear all the harps in Asia play.

Odysseus

He is so delighted with Bacchus' drink
he wants to carouse with his relatives.

Coryphaeus

I see. You'll set an ambush in the woods
and kill him—or push him over a cliff.

Odysseus

No, I had something more subtle in mind.

Coryphaeus

I thought from the first you were sly. What then?

Odysseus

I hope to stop his going on this spree
by saying he shouldn't give his wine away,
but keep it for himself and live in bliss.
Then, as soon as the wine puts him to sleep,
I'll take my sword and sharpen up the trunk
of an olive tree I saw inside the cave.
I'll put it in the coals and when it's caught,
I'll shove it home, dead in the Cyclops' eye,
and blind him. Just like a timber-fitter
whirling his auger around with a belt,
I'll screw the brand in his eye, round and round,
scorch out his eyeball and blind him for good.

Coryphaeus

Bravo! I'm for your plan with all my heart.

Odysseus

And finally, my friends, I'll embark you
and your old father aboard my black ship
and sail full speed away from this place.

Coryphaeus

May I lend a hand at this ritual?
Help hold the pole when you put out his eye?
This is one sacrifice I want to share.

Odysseus

You must. The brand is huge. You all must lift.

Coryphaeus

I could shoulder a hundred wagon-loads
so long as Cyclops died a wretched death!
We'll smoke out his eye like a hornets' nest.

Odysseus

Be quiet now. You know my stratagem.
When I give the word, obey your leaders.
I refuse to save myself and leave my men
trapped inside. I could, of course, escape:
here I am, outside. But I have no right
to abandon my crew and save myself alone.

(*He enters the cave.*)

Chorus

Who'll be first along the brand? Who next?
We'll shove it square in the Cyclops' eye!
We'll rip away his sight.
Quiet.
Shhhh.

(*Polyphemus appears from the cave flanked by Odysseus and Silenus. Odysseus carries the flask and cup, while Silenus holds a pitcher and a mixing-bowl.*)

Here he comes, flat, off-key drunkard,
reeling out of his home in the rock,

braying some wretched tune. Ha!
We'll give him lessons in carousing!

(*Polyphemus stumbles blindly about.*)

A little while: then, perfect blindness!

First semichorus

Happy the man who cries *Evohé!*
stretched out full length and making merry,
for whom the wine keeps flowing,
whose arms are open to his friend!
Lucky man, upon whose bed there blows
the soft bloom of a lovely girl
with gleaming hair, sweet with oil!
who cries: "Who'll open me the door?"

Cyclops

Mamama. Am I crammed with wine!
How I love the fun of a feast!
The hold of my little ship
is stuffed right up to the gunwales!
This marvelous meal reminds me:
I should go feast in the soft spring
with my brothers, the Cyclopes.
Here, here, my friend, hand me the flask.

Second semichorus

O the flash of a handsome Eye!
Handsome himself comes from his house,
Handsome the groom, Handsome the lover!
A soft bride burns for this groom;
she burns in the cool of the cave!
And soon we shall wreathe his head
with a wreath of reddest flowers!

Odysseus

Listen, Cyclops. I've spent a lot of time
with this drink of Bacchus I gave you.

Cyclops
What sort of god is this Bacchus held to be?

Odysseus
Best of all in blessing the lives of men.

Cyclops
(*Belching.*)
At least he makes very tasty belching.

Odysseus
That's the kind of god he is: hurts no one.

Cyclops
How can a god bear to live in a flask?

Odysseus
Wherever you put him, he's quite content.

Cyclops
Gods shouldn't shut themselves up in wine-skins.

Odysseus
What matter, if you like him? Does the flask irk you?

Cyclops
I loathe the flask. The wine is what I like.

Odysseus
Then you should stay here and enjoy yourself.

Cyclops
Shouldn't I share the wine with my brothers?

Odysseus
Keep it to yourself; you'll be more esteemed.

Cyclops
But I'd be more useful if I shared it.

Odysseus
Yes, but carousing often ends in fights.

Cyclops
I'm so drunk nothing could hurt me now.

Odysseus

My dear man, drunkards ought to stay at home.

Cyclops

But the man's a fool who drinks by himself.

Odysseus

It's the wise man who stays home when he's drunk.

Cyclops

What should we do, Silenus? Should I stay home?

Silenus

I would. Why do we want more drinkers, Cyclops?

Cyclops

(*Yawning.*)

Anyway, the ground is soft and the flowers. . . .

Silenus

There's nothing like a drink when the sun is hot.
Lie down there; stretch yourself out on the ground.

(*Cyclops obediently lies down, and furtively Silenus puts the bowl behind his back.*)

Cyclops

There. Why did you put the bowl behind my back?

Silenus

Someone might tip it over.

Cyclops

You wanted
to steal a drink. Put it in the middle.
You there, stranger, tell me what your name is.

Odysseus

Nobody is my name. But how will you reward me?

Cyclops

I will eat you the last of all your crew.

Silenus

That's a fine gift to give your guest, Cyclops.

(*He quickly drains cup.*)

Cyclops

What are you doing? Drinking on the sly?

Silenus

The wine kissed me—for my beautiful eyes.

Cyclops

Watch out. You love the wine; it doesn't love you.

Silenus

Yes, by Zeus, it has a passion for my good looks.

Cyclops

Here, pour me a cupful. But just *pour* it.

Silenus

How is it mixed? Let me taste and see.

(*He takes a quick pull.*)

Cyclops

Damnation! give it here.

Silenus

By Zeus, not before

I see you crowned—

(*He offers Cyclops a wreath of flowers.*)

and have another drink.

(*He empties the cup.*)

Cyclops

This wine-pourer is a cheat!

Silenus

Not at all.

The wine's so good it slides down by itself.
Now wipe yourself off before you drink again.

Cyclops

(*Wiping his face and beard.*)

There. My mouth is clean and so is my beard.

Silenus

Then crook your arm—gracefully now—and drink,
just as you see me drink—and now you don't.

(*He drains cup.*)

Cyclops

Here! What are you doing?

Silenus

Guzzling sweetly.

Cyclops

(*Snatching away the cup and handing it to Odysseus.*)

Here, stranger. Take the flask and pour for me.

Odysseus

At least the wine feels at home in my hand.

Cyclops

Come on, *pour!*

Odysseus

I *am* pouring. Relax, friend.

Cyclops

Relax? That's not so easy when you're drunk.

Odysseus

There, take it up and drink down every drop,
and don't say die until the wine is gone.

Cyclops

Mama. What a wizard the vine must be!

Odysseus

If you drench yourself on a full stomach
and swill your belly, you'll sleep like a log.
Leave a drop, and Bacchus will shrivel you up.

Cyclops

(*Reeling.*)

Whoosh! I can scarcely swim out of this flood.
Pure pleasure! Ohhh. Earth and sky whirling around,
all jumbled up together! Look: I can see
the throne of Zeus and the holy glory
of the gods.

(*The satyrs dance around him suggestively.*)

No, I couldn't make love to you!
The Graces tempt me! My Ganymede here

(*He grabs Silenus.*)

is good enough for me. With him I'll sleep
magnificently. By these Graces, I will!
And anyway, I prefer boys to girls.

Silenus

Am I Zeus' little Ganymede, Cyclops?

Cyclops

You are, by Zeus! The boy I stole from Dardanos!

Silenus

I'm done for, children. Foul things await me.

Cyclops

Sneer at your lover, do you, because he's drunk?

Silenus

It's a bitter wine I'll have to drink now.

(*Cyclops drags off Silenus protesting into the cave.*)

Odysseus

To work, you noble sons of Dionysus!
Our man's inside the cave. In a short while
his belly will heave its foul meal of flesh.
Look, the brand has begun to smoke inside.
We prepared it for just this: to smoke out
the Cyclops' eye. Now you must act like men.

Coryphaeus

Our will is made of unbreakable rock.
But hurry inside before *that* happens
to my father. All is ready out here.

Odysseus

(*Prays.*)

O Hephaestus, ruler over Etna,
free yourself from this vile neighbor of yours!
Sear out his bright eye at one blow! O Sleep,
child of black Night, leap with all your might
on this god-detested beast! And do not,
after our glorious trials at Troy,

betray Odysseus and his crew to death
from a man who cares for neither man nor god.
If you do, we will make a goddess of Chance,
and count her higher than all the other gods!

(*He disappears into the cave.*)

Chorus

Grim tongs shall clutch by the throat
this beast who bolts down his guests.
Fire shall quench the fire of his eye.
The brand, big as a tree, already waits,
waits in the coals.
On, wine, to your work!
Rip out the eye of this raving Cyclops!
Make him regret the day he drank you!
What I want with all my soul to see
is Bacchus, the god who loves the ivy!
Shall I ever see that day?

(*Odysseus reappears from the cave.*)

Odysseus

Quiet, you dogs! By the gods, be quiet!
Hold your tongues. I don't want a man of you
to wink or clear his throat or even breathe.
If we wake up that scourge of evil,
we won't be able to sear out his eye.

(*The satyrs freeze into silence. The following dialogue is conducted entirely in whispers.*)

Coryphaeus

We *are* quiet. Our mouths are locked up tight.

Odysseus

To work then. And grab the brand with both hands
when you enter the cave. The point is red-hot.

Coryphaeus

You should tell us our stations. Who'll be first
on the blazing pole? And then we can all
take our part in searing out the Cyclops' eye.

First parastate
Where we stand, over here by the entrance,
we're too far away to reach his eye.

Second parastate
(*Limping in pain.*)
And just this minute we've gone lame.

First parastate
And we have too. While we were standing here
we sprained our ankles, I don't know how.

Odysseus
Sprained your ankles, standing still?

Second parastate
And my eyes
are full of dust and ashes from somewhere.

Odysseus
What cowards! I won't get any help from you.

Coryphaeus
And because I feel for my back and spine
and don't want to have my teeth knocked out,
I'm a coward, am I? But I can say
a fine Orphic spell that will make the brand
fly of its own accord into the skull
of this one-eyed whelp of Earth and scorch him up.

Odysseus
I knew from that first what sort you were,
and now I know it better. If you're too weak
to lend a hand, at least cheer on my men
and put some heart in them by shouting.
(*He enters the cave.*)

Coryphaeus
We'll shout and this Nobody will run the risks.
We'll fuddle the Cyclops with our shouting.

Chorus

(Dancing excitedly, shouting at the top of its lungs, and imitating the action taking place in the cave.)

Go! Go! As hard as you can!
Push! Thrust! Faster! Burn off
the lashes of the guest-eater!
Smoke him out, burn him out,
the shepherd of Etna!
Twist it! Turn! Careful:
he is hurt and desperate.

(A great shriek from within the cave.)

Cyclops

Owwooooo! My eye is scorched to ashes!

Coryphaeus

Oh song of songs! Sing it for me, Cyclops!

Cyclops

Owwoo! They've murdered me! I'm finished!
But you won't escape this cave to enjoy
your triumph, you contemptible nothings.
I'll stand at the entrance and block it—so.

(Polyphemus appears at the threshold of the cave and stretches his arms across it; his face streams with blood.)

Coryphaeus

What's the matter, Cyclops?

Cyclops

I'm dying.

Coryphaeus

You look terrible.

Cyclops

I feel terrible.

Coryphaeus

Did you get so drunk you fell in the fire?

Cyclops

Nobody wounded me.

Coryphaeus

Then you're not hurt.

Cyclops

Nobody blinded me.

Coryphaeus

Then you're not blind.

Cyclops

Blind as you.

Coryphaeus

How could nobody make you blind?

Cyclops

You mock me. Where is Nobody?

Coryphaeus

Nowhere.

Cyclops

It's the stranger I mean, you fool, the one
who stuffed me full of wine and did me in.

Coryphaeus

(*Sententiously.*)

Wine is tricky; very hard to wrestle with.

Cyclops

By the gods, has he escaped or is he inside?

Coryphaeus

There they are, standing quiet over there,
under cover of the rock.

Cyclops

On which side?

Coryphaeus

On your right.

(*Cyclops leaves the entrance and stumbles with outstretched hands toward the right. Meanwhile the Greeks steal out of the cave.*)

Cyclops

Where?

Coryphaeus

Over against the rock.

Do you have them?

Cyclops

(*Running into a jutting rock.*)

Ouf! Trouble on trouble.

I've split my head.

Coryphaeus

And now they've escaped you.

Cyclops

This way, did you say?

Coryphaeus

No, the other way.

Cyclops

Which way?

Coryphaeus

Turn around. There. On your left.

Cyclops

You're laughing at me in my misery.

Coryphaeus

Not now. There he is in front of you.

Cyclops

Where are you, demon?

(*The Greeks stand at the entrance on the right, a whole length of the stage away from Cyclops.*)

Odysseus

Out of your reach,

Looking after the safety of Odysseus.

Cyclops

What? A new name? Have you changed your name?

Odysseus

Odysseus: the name my father gave me.
You have had to pay for your unholy meal.

I would have done wrong to have fired Troy
but not revenge the murder of my men.

Cyclops

Ah! The old oracle has been fulfilled.
It said that after you had come from Troy,
you would blind me. But you would pay for this,
it said, and wander the seas for many years.

Odysseus

Much I care! What's done is done. As for me,
I'm off to the shore where I'll launch my ship
on the Sicilian shore and sail for home.

(*Exit.*)

Cyclops

Not yet. I'll rip a boulder from this cliff
and crush you and all your crew beneath it.
Blind I may be, but I'll reach the mountain-top
soon enough through the tunnel in the cave.

(*Exits into cave.*)

Chorus

We'll enlist in the crew of Odysseus.
From now our orders come from Bacchus.

HERACLES

Translated by William Arrowsmith

INTRODUCTION TO *HERACLES*

THE *Heracles* of Euripides is seldom assigned a high place in the corpus of extant tragedy. If no one any longer quite accepts Swinburne's description of the play as a "grotesque abortion," the reason is less real disagreement than a habit of respect for the author, supported by a cautious intuition of the play's extraordinary power. Of caution there should be no question. However dislocated in structure the *Heracles* may be, its dramatic power and technical virtuosity are unmistakable. With the possible exception of the *Bacchae*, there is no play into which Euripides has put more of himself and his mature poetic skills than this one. In scene after scene one senses that sureness of movement and precise control of passion which come only with the dramatist's full mastery of his medium. One thinks first of the staggering brutality and shock which erupts in the madness scene, a brutality made all the more terrible by the tenderness which precedes it; or of the great dirge which celebrates the labors of Heracles, and then the confrontation of that ode with the hero's simple "Farewell, my labors"; or, again, of the exquisite ode in praise of youth and the service of the Muses, poetry tense with the full pressure of the poet's life behind it; and, last of all, that anguished exchange between Theseus and Heracles in which the hero, broken by his suffering, weak, reduced to his final humanity, comes on his greatest heroism, surely one of the most poignant codas in Greek tragedy.

Technically, at least, it is a brilliant performance, boldness of dramatic stroke and vigor of invention everywhere visible, but particularly in the brisk counterpoint of peripeties on which the tragedy turns, wheeling over and over as one action pivots to its opposite, or, juxtaposed against a sudden illumination, is as suddenly shattered and annulled. Through theme after theme, with perfect tact of tempo and placing, the reversals crowd, taking each motif a further turn of the wheel. Thus the first action of the play, slow, conventional, overwhelmed by the weakness of its characters, creates out of desperation a sudden and time-honored theodicy. The wheel turns, and a violent irruption of the irrational smashes all theodicy; then, in the last swing, both irrational and theodicy are alike undone in the hero's enormous leap to an illusion of order in divinity, an assertion which he maintains squarely in the teeth of his experience. The savior who suddenly turns destroyer is in turn saved from self-destruction by the man he had earlier saved from Hades. The hero is reduced to his humanity as the condition of his heroism. Throughout the tragedy, gathering momentum by contrast, runs the rhythm of its minor terms: first despair, then hope, then again despair, and finally an endurance deeper than either; age and youth, weakness and strength, both pairs resolved in the condition that makes them one. Schematic, brilliant, savagely broken, the *Heracles* is a play ot great power and, with the exception of the *Orestes*, the most violent structural tour-de-force in Greek tragedy.

It is this very dislocation, this virtuosity and violence in the play's structure, which more than anything else has injured its reputation and hindered reappraisal. Given Aristotelian standards of judgment (and Aristotle even today affects dramatic criticism at a profound level), the play's dislocation could not but appear either pointless or gratuitous; for at almost every conceivable point the play is in flat contradiction to the principles of the *Poetics*. Thus Heracles has no visible *hamartia;* if he falls, he falls for no flaw of his own nature or failure of judgment, but as the innocent victim of divine brutality. And still worse, the play exhibits not at all that deep, necessitous *propter hoc* connection between its parts, which for Aristotle constituted the right structure of tragedy.[1] With almost one voice both critics and scholars from Aristotle to the present have reported the dislocation of the play as an insuperable blemish. The *Heracles*, they say, is "broken-backed,"[2] a tragedy that "falls so clearly into two parts that we cannot view it as a work of art."[3] But in so saying, they report, I think, as much their own outraged Aristotelianism as the obvious facts of the play's structure.

1. *Poetics* 1452^{a}. 20.

2. Gilbert Murray, *Greek Studies*, p. 112.

3. Gilbert Norwood, *Greek Tragedy*, p. 229.

Beyond question the play falls starkly into two discrete but continuous actions, and between these two actions there is neither causal necessity nor even probability: the second action follows but by no means arises out of the first. Through the close of the chorus which celebrates the slaying of Lycus (l. 814), we have one complete action as conventional in movement as it is in subject: a familiar tableau of suppliants, their cruel antagonist, an *agōn* in which the tormentor is slain by the savior, and a closing hymn in praise of the hero and the vindicated justice of the gods. This melodramatic action is shattered by the appearance of Madness and Iris, and the play, in violation of all probability, careens around to commence a wholly new action. Utterly unexpected and without causal ground in the first part of the play, the madness of Heracles and the murder of his wife and children are simply set down in glaring contrast to the preceding action. Against theodicy is put the hideous proof of divine injustice; against the greatness and piety and *aretē* of Heracles in the first action is placed the terrible reward of heroism in the second; against the asserted peace and calm and domestic tenderness which closes the first action is set the utter annihilation of all moral order in the second. The result is a structure in which two apparently autonomous actions are jammed savagely against each other in almost total contradiction, with no attempt to minimize or even modulate the profound formal rift.

That rift is, of course, deliberate; nothing, in fact, has been omitted which might support the effect of total shock in this reversal. Moreover, even a cursory review of the material which Euripides used for his tragedy shows how carefully that material has been ordered to effect, rather than obviate, this dislocation of structure.

Old tradition told of Hera's persecution of Heracles because of her jealousy of Zeus's amour with Heracles' mother, Alcmene. It also told how Heracles, driven mad by Hera, slew his sons and would also have killed his father, Amphitryon, had not Athene intervened and knocked the raging hero unconscious with a stone. For the most part Euripides has retained these traditions, but with this great difference: whereas in the common tradition the great labors of

Heracles were undertaken in penance for the murder of the children, Euripides has transposed the murders to the time just after the completion of the labors, the height of Heracles' career. Because Heracles at the very moment of his fall is at his greatest, the hideousness of Hera's revenge is sharply underscored and its abrupt, tragic senselessness stressed. The dramatist, that is, has ordered his material in such a way as to achieve precisely that dislocation which the play's structure exhibits. Nor is this all. Because Euripides has transposed the labors and the murders, he has been forced to invent a new motive for the labors. This is the motive of filial piety: Heracles undertook his labors in order to win back the country from which Amphitryon had been exiled for the murder of Electryon. Thus at the same time that Euripides freely invents in order to fill the gap caused by the original transposition, he also subtly humanizes his hero in preparation for the conversion which is the heart of the second action.

Tradition also told of Heracles' suicide on Mt. Oeta (cf. Sophocles' *Trachiniae*) and how after death the hero was translated to heaven and given everlasting youth in the person of Hebe. This entire saga is suppressed in the Euripidean version, but the very fact of its suppression informs the *Heracles* throughout, pointing up the direction of the action against what has been excluded. Thus Heracles, far from being deified in Euripides, is humanized[4] as the condition of his heroism. And far from committing suicide, the Euripidean Heracles discovers his greatest nobility in refusing to die and choosing life. If, again in the older tradition, Heracles married Hebe (i.e., youth) and so won everlasting life, in the Euripidean play Hebe is present to the action as nothing more than an impossible anguished reminder of mortal necessity and the haunting image of what in a universe not fatally flawed might have been the reward of human

4. In the humanization of Heracles, Euripides returns to the oldest of all extant Heracles traditions, the Homeric, in which Heracles too had to die. Cf. *Iliad* xviii. 115 ff.: "Not even the great Heracles escaped death, though he was dear to the lord Zeus, the son of Cronus, but the common fate brought him down, and the grievous wrath of Hera." In literature of the historical period this tradition has almost everywhere been eclipsed by the deified Heracles, a version which begins also with Homer (cf. *Odyssey* xi. 601 ff.).

virtue (cf. 637–72). Similarly, the suppression of the deification motif sharpens the courageous endurance of mankind under its necessities in contrast with the happiness of the amoral gods. Deification is replaced by the closest thing to Olympus this world can offer —honored asylum at Athens. For this reason Theseus is introduced as the representative of Athenian humanity to rescue and annex to Athens the greatest Dorian hero.

By deployment of his material Euripides has structured his play into two parallel actions divided by a peripety whose purpose is more to stress the break than to bridge it. If the *Heracles* is broken, the dislocation is at least deliberate, and as such it is clearly consistent with Euripides' practice elsewhere: in the two actions of the *Hecuba*, the double plot of the *Hippolytus*, the episodic *Trojan Women* or *Phoenissae*, the broken *Andromache*, and the dislocated *Electra*. But even more violently than these plays the *Heracles* insists on the irreparable rift in its structure and invites us by its great power to discover what nonetheless makes it one play. It is right that our perception of power in literature should lead us more deeply into the order and disorder created or invoked.

Despite the fact that the first action is entirely free invention, it is important to see how conventional the treatment is. In the shaping of the characters, in their attributes and motives, in the theology and received values to which the action appeals, convention is everywhere visible. Character is essentially static, the action as a whole leached of any really tragic movement. All the emotional stops of a melodramatic situation have been pulled: we move from the despair of the helpless family to the sudden coming of the savior hero to the triumphant final diapason of vindicated divine justice. The characters are only lightly dubbed in, certainly no more so than is necessary to maintain the illusion that these are real people in a situation of unqualified peril. If the action is not quite trite, it is at least customary and predictable, so predictable in fact that it might be regarded as a parody of a standard tragic movement. Certainly no one familiar with Euripides' practice can doubt that the comfortable theodicy which closes the action has been written tongue-in-cheek or is somehow surely riding for a fall. And insensibly the impression of purely tragic power in the second action, although based on an analogous plot, undercuts the first action and exposes its conventionality.

What is true of the first action as a whole is also true of the Heracles of the first action. The traditional *données* which compose his figure have for the most part been carefully preserved; if Heracles is not here the beefeater of comedy or the ruddy sensualist of the *Alcestis*, he is recognizably the familiar culture-hero of Dorian and Boeotian tradition: strong, courageous, noble, self-sufficient, carrying on his back all the aristocratic *aretē* of the moralized tradition of Pindar. Thus the grossnesses or cruelties or philandering which tradition sometimes ascribed to him (cf. again the *Trachiniae*) have been stripped away. In domestic life he is a devoted son, a loyal husband, and a fond father; in civil life he is the just king, the enemy of *hybris*, the champion of the helpless, and the loyal servant of the gods. His civilizing labors on behalf of mankind are accepted as literal truths, and the curious ambiguity in tradition which made Heracles the son of two fathers, Zeus and Amphitryon, is maintained. His heroism is based upon his strength and is essentially outward, but nonetheless valid, or at least valid enough for the muted reality of the first action.

Against this background, the second action breaks with tragic force and striking transformations, showing first the conquering hero, the *kallinikos*, reduced to tears, helpless, dependent, and in love, stripped of that outward strength which until now had exempted him from normal human necessity, and discovering both his common ground with men and a new internalized moral courage. This Heracles is not merely untraditional; he is almost inconceivable in traditional perspective, and he is tragic where the earlier Heracles was merely noble. The point to be insisted upon here is the distance at every point between the two actions. We have here moved a whole world away from the simple virtues and theodicy of the first action, as the new role and courage of the hero undercut everything the play has created up to now. The world of the given, the reality of "things as they are said to be," withers and is replaced, not by a mere contradiction, but by a new tragic myth invoking new values and grounded in a sterner reality. What audience, especially a Greek one, could have recognized in that broken, almost domestic, Heracles fighting back his tears, the familiar and austere culture-hero of received tradition?

We have, then, two savagely different actions, one conventional and the other set in a world where tradition is dumb and conduct uncharted, placed harshly in contrast. The peripety which separates them is the dramatist's means of expressing symbolically the fatal disorder of the moral universe, and also the device by which the heroism of the second action is forced up, through an utter transformation of assumed reality. The whole play exhibits, as though on two plateaus, a *conversion* of reality. A story or legend derived from received beliefs—the world of myth and the corpus of "things as they are said to be"—is suddenly in all of its parts, terms, characters, and the values it invokes *converted* under dramatic pressure to another phase of reality. What we get is something like a dramatic mutation of received reality, and the leap the play makes between the phases or plateaus of its two realities is meant to correspond in force and vividness and apparent unpredictability to mutations in the physical world. It is this violence in the conversion of reality that explains the wrenching dislocation of Euripidean drama from an Aristotelian point of view and the lack of apparent connection between the parts of the play. The play pivots on two seemingly incompatible realities, and if it insists on the greater reality of what has been created over what has been received, it does so, not by denying reality to receive reality, but by subtly displacing it in the transfiguration of its terms.

Thus, point for point in the *Heracles*, each of the terms—the qualities, situation, characters—that was appropriate to the Heracles of tradition is transformed and displaced. If in the first action both Zeus and Amphitryon are the fathers of Heracles, in the second action Amphitryon becomes Heracles' "real" father, not by the fact of conception, but by the greater fact of love, *philia*. In the first action Heracles literally decended to a literal Hades; in the second action this literal descent is transfigured in the refusal to die and the courage which, under an intolerable necessity, perseveres. There is a hint, moreover, that the old Hades of the poets with its Cerberus, Sisyphus, and torments is transformed in the second part into the Hades within, here and now, internalized as Heracles himself declares, "And I am like Ixion, forever chained to a flying wheel." So too the old labors appear to be replaced by the metaphorical sense of the imposed labors of human life and the cost of civilization, while the goddess Hera, who in legend made Heracles mad, passes almost insensibly into a hovering symbol of all those irrational and random necessities which the Greek and the play call *Tyche*, and which we limply translate as "Fortune" or "necessity."

All of these conversions replace and dislodge the reality of the first action by transfiguring it at every point. The first action in the light of the second is neither false nor unreal, but inadequate. Through the force of contrast with its own conversion, it comes to seem obsolete, naïve, or even humdrum, much as fresh conviction formed under *peine forte et dure* insensibly makes the conviction it replaces callow or jejune in comparison. Under the changed light of experience and the pattern it imposes, what was once taken for reality comes to seem illusion at best: true while held as true, but with widened experience, discovered inadequate. What we see is less the contradiction between the two opposed realities than the counterpointed relation of their development, the way in which, under the blow of suffering and insight, one reality is made to yield a further one, each geared to its appropriate experience. We begin with a familiar and conventional world, operating from familiar motives among accepted though outmoded values; by the time the play closes, characters, motives, and values have all been pushed to the very frontiers of reality.

But if in this context of conversion the conventional first action is undercut and dislodged by the tragic second action, the first action also helps to inform the second and to anticipate its discoveries. Thus Heracles' desperation after his madness is paralleled by his family's desperation in the first part; what they say and do there is meant to be applied with full force to his situation later. If courage for them lies in the nobility with which they accept the necessity of death, nobility for Heracles lies in the courage with which he accepts his life as his necessity, for, in Amphitryon's words:

> To persevere, trusting in what hopes he has,
> is courage in a man. The coward despairs [ll. 105–6].

If Amphitryon in the first action possesses a "useless" life (l. 42) by virtue of extreme old age and weakness, Heracles later comes to possess the same "useless" life (l. 1302), and so both meet on the grounds of their common condition. Similarly the chorus speaks of its own necessity, old age, as "a weight more heavy than Aetna's rocks, / hiding in darkness / the light of my eyes" (ll. 639–41); that same darkness, not as age but as grief, lies later on the eyes of Heracles (ll. 1140, 1159, 1198, 1104–5, 1216, 1226ff.), the dark night of his soul. And just as the chorus in the first action finds the hope of its life in poetry and perseveres in the Muses' service, so Theseus uncovers Heracles to the sun and shows him the hope in *philia* which enables him to live. So too when Heracles, self-sufficient and independent, leads his children into the palace before his madness, he draws them behind him like little boats in tow (*epholkidas*); but at the end of the play Heracles, broken, in love and dependent, follows in Theseus' wake to Athens like a little boat in tow (*epholkides*). The same implicit counterpoint between the two actions explains in part, I think, the unqualified villainy of Lycus. Balancing the corruption of human power and brutality (*amathia*) in him, comes the abuse of divine power in Hera—a far more heinous abuse, since divine cruelty is a fortiori worse than human brutality. Beyond this, I suspect, we are intended to see correspondence again in the physical death which Lycus meets at Heracles' hands and the spiritual annihilation of Hera which is the consequence of Heracles' great speech on the gods (ll. 1340–46). But throughout the play, in metaphor, in contrast of whole scenes, in visual imagery, the two actions are paralleled at point after point. Below the level of the violent structural dislocation of the play runs a constant crisscross of reference, comment, and contrast throwing single words or themes into sharp relief in continuous qualification of the whole action. In the perception of this continuous conversion of the play's terms lies the understanding of its movement and unity.

Point by point the deepest motive of the play is to bring Heracles to the place where he shares for the first time common ground with the others, all of whom, like him, are laid under the heavy yoke of necessity but lack that enormous physical strength which has hitherto exempted him. But if he must come to share that yoke with them, if he is reduced to his humanity as the condition of the only heroism that counts, he also comes to know for the first time that other, and redeeming, yoke of love, *philia*, which alone makes necessity endurable. For the *Heracles* is a play which imposes suffering upon men as their tragic condition, but it also discovers a courage equal to that necessity, a courage founded on love. We witness in the play a conversion of heroism whose model is Heracles, and the heart of that conversion lies in the hero's passage in suffering from the outworn courage of outward physical strength to a new internal courage, without exemption now but with the addition of love and perseverance against an intolerable necessity.

Love is the hope, the *elpis*, which permits him to endure, and his discovery of that hope keeps step with his knowledge of anguish. He survives by virtue of love, for love lies close to, if it does not usurp, the instinct for survival. At the close of the play we see Heracles assert the dignity of his grief against the reproaches of a Theseus who, for all his generosity, is still rooted in the old heroism and no longer understands. Having claimed the dignity of his new courage, Heracles can without weakness or loss of tragic stature make plain the wreck of his life and his own dependent helplessness: strong but also weak, in need and in love, a hero at every point.

Heracles comes through suffering, then, to occupy the ground where Megara, Amphitryon, and the chorus stood earlier. Their nobility provides a standard by which to measure his heroism, first challenging it and then being surpassed by it. But nothing in Heracles is diminished because Megara and Amphitryon have set the example he must follow, and know already what he must learn. Their very weakness has set them close to necessity, while Heracles' *aretē* has been so prodigiously developed toward physical strength that nothing short of the greatest moral courage is required for him to survive his necessity. He rises and keeps on rising to his sufferings with an enormous range of spirit that in the end leaves even the unconventional Theseus far behind him. It is this ability to rise that makes him great as much as the overwhelming anguish of the necessity that confronts him. What counts in the end is not the disparity between Heracles' courage and necessity and the courage of the others, but the fact that they all—Megara, Amphitryon, the chorus, and Heracles—meet on the common ground of their condition and discover both courage and hope in the community of weakness and love.

What, finally, are we to make of Hera and that crucial speech of Heracles on the nature of the gods (ll. 1340–46)? That it was Hera who made Heracles mad was, as we have seen, an essential part of Euripides' legendary material. But the consequence of Heracles' speech is apparently to deny that the actions of the gods could in fact be such as they are dramatized to be. Alternatively Heracles appears to deny the reality of the experience out of which he makes the speech in the first place. For to say that "if god is truly god, then he is perfect, / lacking nothing" is clearly to invalidate Hera's claim to divinity, or to deny his own experience of Hera's hatred.

The sentiment is, to be sure, Euripidean, a familiar refusal to believe the old legends which represent the gods as subject to human passions, and a discountenance of the familiar fifth-century notion that immoral conduct could be sanctioned by an appeal to divine conduct as recounted in poetry. But merely because the lines are Euripidean in thought, their effect for the play should not be glozed away as mere inconsistencies or as an undramatic intrusion of the dramatist *in propria persona*. For to say that divine adultery, tyranny, and misconduct are all "the wretched tales of poets" is a direct and unmistakable challenge not only to the Hera of the play, but to the whole Olympian system.

The consequences of Heracles' words for the play are, I suggest, this: that the story of Hera's action as dramatized is true enough, but the Hera who afflicts Heracles as she does thereby renounces any claim to the kind of divinity which Heracles asserts. This conclusion is, I think, supported by Euripides' practice elsewhere and also by the language of the play. Like the *Hippolytus* with Aphrodite and the *Bacchae* with Dionysus, the *Heracles* does two things with Hera: it first dramatizes the legend which contains her action as incredible in a goddess,[5] and then, having shown *and* asserted its incredibility, it converts her into a hovering symbol of all the unknown and unknowable forces which compel Heracles and men to suffer tragically and without cause or sense. As Dionysus is a complex symbol for the forces of life, amoral and necessitous, so Hera comprehends all the principles of peripety and change and random necessity. She is not Hera, but "Hera," a name given her for the want of a name, but loosely what the Greeks meant by *Tyche*, the lady of necessity and reversal. In asserting this "Hera" as the consequence of his own speech, Heracles annihilates the old Olympian Hera as a goddess, but also converts her into that demonic and terribly real power of his own necessity. The tragedy of Heracles is both true and real, but it is no longer the traditional story, nor is Heracles the same man, nor Hera the same goddess. And it is to confirm this conversion that Heracles a few lines later (l. 1357) concludes: "And now, I see, I must serve necessity (*tyche*)." So too in his last reference to Hera he hints at the conversion by significantly juxtaposing both *tyche* and the name of Hera, claiming that "we all have been struck down by one *tyche* of Hera" (l. 1393).[6] And, if this were not enough, the play's overwhelming preoccupation with peripety as theme and as dislocation in structure would confirm the conversion. This, I think, is what we should expect, that the conversion of the old legend of Heracles and his old nobility into a new myth should be accompanied by the conversion of his necessity as well. To alter his old heroism without also altering the source of his suffering would be to cripple the conversion at the crucial point. It would obscure, that is, the fact that Heracles, though broken by necessity, still wins the moral victory over the power that ruins him, earning for himself

5. Cf. ll. 1307–10 where Heracles asks: "Who could offer prayers to such a goddess? Jealous of Zeus for a mortal woman's sake, she has destroyed Hellas' greatest friend, though he was guiltless."

6. Cf. ll. 1314, 1349, 1396, as well as the significant disjunction, "mastered by Hera or by necessity" in Amphitryon's speech at l. 20.

and men in a different sense the victory claimed by Amphitryon over Zeus earlier:

And I, mere man, am nobler than you, a great god [l. 342].

He claims a courage more than equal to his condition and can therefore claim the dignity of his grief.

Heracles is no Aristotelian hero, nor is the play an Aristotelian tragedy; yet the *Heracles* is a great tragedy and Heracles himself a great tragic hero. The gulf between Euripides and Aristotle on the issues here is a great and permanent one that deserves to be stressed. For Aristotle a tragic fall is grounded in a consistent and harmonious sense of man's responsibility for his nature and his actions: when the hero falls, he falls for his own failure, and behind the rightness of his fall, working both pity and fear by the precise and relentless nature of its operations, stands the order which society and a god-informed world impose upon the individual. What the law requires the gods require too, and so the Aristotelian play portrays, like an image of human life, the individual torn and suffering between his nature and an objective world-order. In Euripides it is otherwise; here the suffering of the individual under his necessity may have no such rightness, or even none at all, as in the *Heracles*. The world-order of the gods as reflected in "things as they are said to be" is either incredible or an indictment of that order, and if it imposes necessities unjustly upon a man, the very courage with which he endures makes him tragic and gives him the moral victory over his own fate. Similarly with society: for society may be no less corrupt than the "gods" and as unjust in the necessities it imposes. Euripides, that is, preserves the disorder of actual experience, measuring its horror against the unrequited illusion of order which sustains human beings. His image of tragic humanity is earned less in the conflict between the individual's nature and the necessities imposed by a higher order than in the conflict between the individual and his own internalized necessities. In the *Heracles*, at least, it is the very innocence of the hero which condemns the "gods" who make him mad; but because the gods are first rendered incredible and then transformed into a collective symbol for all the random, senseless operations of necessity in human life, the courage with which the hero meets his fate and asserts a moral order beyond his own experience is just as tragic and just as significant as that of Oedipus.

Date and Circumstances

The *Heracles* is undated, and no attempt to date the play to any one year can be regarded as wholly successful. The most favored date is one close to 424–423. It has been held that the heavy emphasis throughout the play upon old age in connection with military service, particularly the bitter first strophe of the second *stasimion* (ll. 637 ff.), represents a direct personal intrusion of the poet on having reached his sixtieth year (when he would have been exempt from further military service). On such a theory the date of the play would be 424–423. Similarly, the disproportionate debate on the bow (ll. 188 ff.) is interpreted as an overt reference to the Athenian success at Sphakteria in 425—a victory due largely to bowmen—or to the disastrous failure to employ archers in the hoplite defeat at Delium in 424. The reference to Delian maidens (ll. 687 ff.) is taken as a remembrance of the establishment of the quiquennial *Deliades* in Athens in 425.

But no one of these suggestions, nor even their ensemble, can be regarded as decisive. The strongest argument for a later date is one given by stylistic and metrical tests, generally rather accurate for Euripides. These tend to place the play in the group of dramas which directly follow the Archidamian War, or about 418–416.

It is my opinion that the metrical tests are supported in their results by the general political tone of the play, with its sharp emphasis upon factional strife and its concern with the badge of true nobility. Further, the reconciliation between Sparta and Athens which is suggested in Theseus' domiciling of Heracles in Athens would seem to suggest (though it need not) a period in which reconciliation between Athens and Sparta was possible. Such reconciliation was a possibility only, I believe, in the period between the close of the Archidamian War in 421 and the aggressive anti-Spartan policy of Alcibiades which cluminated in the Athenian-Argive defeat at

Mantinea in 418. It is only against such a background as this, when all major parties in the Peloponnesian War were attempting abortive realignments, when peace must have appeared to be at least a remote possibility to contemporaries, that the lines of Megara (ll. 474–79) can be made to yield good sense. If so, the death of the children who embody the peaceful hopes of a united Hellas (ll. 135–37) must mean the renewal of conflict. A renewal of conflict must have seemed the certain consequence of Alcibiades' policies in 418, whereas in the years just previous an alliance between Athens and Sparta must have excited real hopes of an enduring peace.

Text

The basis of this translation is the Oxford text of Gilbert Murray, though it has often been supplemented by others,[1] chiefly the brilliant edition of Leon Parmentier in the Budé series.[2] Upon a few occasions I have also adopted the emendations proposed by Wilamowitz. The notes on the translation are not designed to indicate all departures from the Murray text (nor even to mark the numerous occasions on which I preferred the reading of the manuscripts over modern emendations),[3] but to amplify variations or emendations

1. L. 496: cf. D. S. Robertson, "Euripides, *H.F. 497 ff.*," *C.R.* LII (1938), 50–51.

2. L. 1241: "Then where it touches heaven, I shall strike." I adopt here the emendation of Parmentier and read *kai thenein* for *katthanein*. Since Theseus at l. 1246 asks Heracles what he will do and where his passion sweeps him, and Heracles replies in the following line that he will die, it seems plausible that *katthanein* here is a simple copyist's mistake for the less familiar *kai thenein*. And, as Parmentier remarks, the line as emended pivots on a play with the word *haptēi* in the preceding line (l. 1240). It is also more likely that Theseus in l. 1242 would take *thenein* as a threat against the gods than he would the precise self-directed *katthanein*. See L. Parmentier, *Revue de philologie*, XLIV (1920), 161.

3. L. 1351: *Enkarterēsō thanaton* ("I shall prevail against death"). *Thanaton* is here the reading of the manuscripts and, to some degree, it is supported by the identical phrase at *Andromache* l. 262 (though in each case the contextual meaning is different). Murray, following Wecklein and Wilamowitz, however, has altered *thanaton* to *bioton* (life).

So far as the quality of affirmation is concerned here, however, there is little difference between *thanaton* and *bioton*. Both imply the affirmative decision to bear necessity by living; clarity is unaffected by either reading. Though to prevail against life (in the sense of "persevering") may be more forceful than to prevail against death (in the

whose use appeared to me to bear upon the interpretation of the whole play. Lines which are bracketed indicate probable interpolations.

---

sense of resisting the temptation to die), it seems to me that the imagery of the play is decisive for *thanaton*. In Heracles' words here, that is, we have the metaphorical (but also realistic) equivalent of the mythical descent to Hades and the conquest of death it signifies. Heracles has in his sufferings been to Hades and at death's door; he now wrestles with his death as myth once imagined him as wrestling for Cerberus. And just as the chorus once (ll. 655 ff.) hoped that the noble man might receive a double life as a reward of *aretē*, in this line we see the vindication of *aretē* in the internalized *eugeneia* which conquers death.

CHARACTERS

Amphitryon, father of Heracles

Megara, wife of Heracles

Chorus of old men of Thebes

Lycus, usurper of the throne of Thebes

Heracles

Iris, messenger of the gods

Madness

Messenger

Theseus, king of Athens

For Robert and Renée Preyer
zeugos ge philion

HERACLES

SCENE: *Before the palace of Heracles at Thebes. In the foreground is the altar of Zeus. On its steps, in the posture of suppliants, sit the aged Amphitryon, Megara, and her three small sons. Amphitryon rises and speaks the prologue.*

Amphitryon

What mortal lives who has not heard this name—
Amphitryon of Argos, who shared his wife
with Zeus? I am he: son of Alcaeus
Perseus' son, but father of Heracles.
Here I settled, in this Thebes, where once the earth
was sown with dragonteeth and sprouted men;
and Ares saved a few that they might people
Cadmus' city with their children's children.
From these sown men Creon was descended,
son of Menoeceus and our late king.
This lady is Megara, Creon's daughter,
for whose wedding once all Thebes shrilled
to flutes and songs as she was led, a bride,
home to his father's halls by Heracles.
Then my son left home, left Megara and kin,
hoping to recover the plain of Argos
and those gigantic walls from which I fled
to Thebes, because I killed Electryon.
He hoped to win me back my native land
and so alleviate my grief. And therefore,
mastered by Hera or by necessity,

he promised to Eurystheus a vast price
for our return: to civilize the world.
When all his other labors had been done,
he undertook the last: descended down
to Hades through the jaws of Taenarus
to hale back up to the light of day
the triple-bodied dog.
He has not come back.
Here in Thebes the legend goes that once
a certain Lycus married Dirce, our queen,
and ruled this city with its seven gates
before the twins of Zeus, those "white colts,"
Amphion and Zethus, ruled the land.
This Lycus' namesake and descendant,
no native Theban but Euboean-born,
attacked our city, sick with civil war,
murdered Creon and usurped his throne.
And now our marriage-bond with Creon's house
has proved in fact to be our greatest ill.
For since my son is gone beneath the earth,
this upstart tyrant, Lycus, plans to kill
the wife and sons of Heracles—and me,
so old and useless, that I scarcely count—
blotting murder with more, lest these boys
grown to men, someday revenge their mother's house.
My son, when he descended to the darkness
underground, left me here, appointing me
both nurse and guardian of his little sons.
Now, to keep these heirs of Heracles from death,
their mother and I in supplication
kneeled to Zeus the Savior at this altar,
established by the prowess of my son,
the trophy of his conquering spear
and monument of Minyan victory.
Here we sit, in utter destitution,

lacking food, water, and clothing; having no beds
but the bare earth beneath our bodies;
barred from our house, empty of hope.
And of our friends, some prove no friends at all,
while those still true are powerless to help.
This is what misfortune means among mankind;
upon no man who wished me well at all,
could I wish this acid test of friends might fall.

Megara

Old man, marshal of our famous Theban arms,
who once destroyed the city of the Taphians,
how dark are all the ways of god to man!
Prosperity was my inheritance:
I had a father who could boast of wealth,
who had such power as makes the long spears
leap with greed against its proud possessor—
a father, blessed with children, who gave me
in glorious marriage to your Heracles.
But now his glory is gone down in death,
and you and I, old man, shall soon be dead,
and with us, these small sons of Heracles
whom I ward and nestle underwing.
First one, then another, bursts in tears,
and asks: "Mother, where has Father gone?
What is he doing? When will he come back?"
Then, too small to understand, they ask again
for "Father." I put them off with stories;
but when the hinges creak, they all leap up
to run and throw themselves at their father's feet.
Is there any hope? What chance of rescue
do we have, old man? We look to you.
The border is impassable by stealth;
sentries have been set on every road;
all hope that friends might rescue us is gone.

So tell me now if you have any plan,
or if you have resigned yourself to death.

Amphitryon

My child, I find it hard in such a case
to give advice offhand without hard thought.
We are weak, and weakness can only wait.

Megara

Wait for worse? Do you love life so much?

Amphitryon

I love it even now. I love its hopes.

Megara

And I. But hope is of things possible.

Amphitryon

A cure may come in wearing out the time.

Megara

It is the time between that tortures me.

Amphitryon

Even now, out of our very evils,
for you and me a better wind may blow.
My son, your husband, still may come. Be calm;
dry the living springs of tears that fill
your children's eyes. Console them with stories,
those sweet thieves of wretched make-believe.
Human misery must somewhere have a stop:
there is no wind that always blows a storm;
great good fortune comes to failure in the end.
All is change; all yields its place and goes;
to persevere, trusting in what hopes he has,
is courage in a man. The coward despairs.

(*Enter the Chorus of old men of Thebes. They walk painfully, leaning upon their staffs.*)

Chorus

STROPHE

Leaning on our staffs we come
to the vaulted halls and the old man's bed,
our song the dirge of the dying swan,
ourselves mere words, ghosts that walk
in the visions of night,
trembling with age,
trembling to help.
O children, fatherless sons,
old man and wretched wife
who mourn your lord in Hades!

ANTISTROPHE

Do not falter. Drag your weary feet
onward like the colt that, yoked and slow,
tugs uphill, on rock, the heavy wain.
If any man should fall,
support him with your hands,
age hold up his years
as once when he was young
he supported his peers
in the toils of war
and was no blot on his country's fame.

EPODE

Look how the children's eyes
flash forth like their father's!
Misfortune has not left them,
nor has loveliness.
O Hellas, Hellas,
losing these boys,
what allies you lose!
No more. Look: I see my country's tyrant,
Lycus, approaching the palace.

(*Enter Lycus with attendants.*)

Lycus

You there,
father of Heracles, and you, his wife:
allow me one question. And you must allow it:
I am the power here; I ask what I wish.
How long will you seek to prolong your lives?
What hope have you? What could prevent your death?
Or do you think the father of these boys
who lies dead with Hades will still come back?
How shabbily you suffer when you both must die—
you who filled all Hellas with your hollow boasts
that Zeus was partner in your son's conception;
and you, that you were wife of the noblest man!
What was so prodigious in your husband's deeds?
Because he killed a hydra in a marsh?
Or the Nemean lion? They were trapped in nets,
not strangled, as he claims, with his bare hands.
Are these your arguments? Because of this,
you say, the sons of Heracles should live—
a man who, coward in everything else,
made his reputation fighting beasts,
who never buckled shield upon his arm,
never came near a spear, but held a bow,
the coward's weapon, handy to run away?
The bow is no proof of manly courage;
no, your real man stands firm in the ranks
and dares to face the gash the spear may make.
My policy, old man, is not mere cruelty;
call it caution. I am well aware
that I killed Creon and usurped his throne.
It does not suit my wishes that these boys
go free to take their grown revenge on me.

Amphitryon

Let Zeus act to guard his interest in his son.
For my part, Heracles, I have but words
to prove this man's gross ignorance of you.

I cannot bear that you should be abused.
First for his slander, for such I call it
when you are called a coward, Heracles.
I call upon the gods to bear me witness:
that thunder of Zeus, his chariot
in which you rode, stabbing with winged shafts
the breasts of the giant spawn of earth,
and raised the victory-cry with the gods!
Go to Pholoë and see the centaurs,
go ask them, those four-legged monsters,
what man they judge to be the bravest,
if not my son, whose courage you call sham.
Go ask Abantian Dirphys which bore you:
it will not praise you. You have never done
one brave deed your fatherland could cite.
You sneer at that wise invention, the bow.
Listen to me and learn what wisdom is.
Your spearsman is the slave of his weapons;
unless his comrades in the ranks fight well,
then he dies, killed by their cowardice;
and once his spear, his sole defense, is smashed,
he has no means of warding death away.
But the man whose hands know how to aim the bow,
holds the one best weapon: a thousand arrows shot,
he still has more to guard himself from death.
He stands far off, shooting at foes who see
only the wound the unseen arrow plows,
while he himself, his body unexposed,
lies screened and safe. This is best in war:
to preserve yourself and to hurt your foe
unless he stands secure, beyond your range.
Such are my arguments, squarely opposed
to yours on every point at issue here.
What will you achieve by killing these boys?
How have they hurt you? Yet I grant you wise
in one respect: being base yourself,

you fear the children of a noble man.
Still, this goes hard with us, that we must die
to prove your cowardice, a fate which you
might better suffer at our better hands,
if the mind of Zeus intended justice here.
But if the sceptre is what you desire,
then let us go as exiles from the land.
But beware of force, lest you suffer it,
when god swings round again with veering wind.
O country of Cadmus, on you too
my reproaches fall! Is this your vigil
for the sons of Heracles? For Heracles,
who single-handed fought your Minyan foe
and made Thebes see once more with free men's eyes?
No more can I praise Hellas, nor be still,
finding her so craven toward my son:
with sword, spear, and fire she should have come
to help these boys in gratitude to him,
for all his labors clearing land and sea.
Poor children, both Thebes and Hellas fail you.
And so you turn to me, a weak old man,
nothing more now than a jawing of words,
forsaken by that strength I used to have,
left only with this trembling husk of age.
But if my youth and strength could come again,
I'd take my spear and bloody your brown hair
until you ran beyond the bounds of Atlas,
trying, coward, to outrun my spear!

Chorus

There is a source of speech in all brave men
which does not fail, although the tongue be slow.

Lycus

Go on, rant, pile up your tower of words!
My actions, not my words, shall answer your abuse.

(*Turning to his attendants.*)

Go, men, to Helicon and Parnassus:
tell the woodsmen there to chop up oaken logs
and haul them to the city. Then pile your wood
around the altar here on every side,
and let it blaze. Burn them all alive
until they learn the dead man rules no more;
that I, and I alone, am the power here.
But you old men, for this defiance,
you shall mourn the sons of Heracles
and each disaster that devours this house,
each separate grief, until you learn
you are only slaves; I am the master.

Chorus

O sons of earth, men whom Ares sowed,
teeth he tore from the dragon's foaming jaw,
up, up with these staffs that prop our arms
and batter the skull of this godless man,
no Theban, but an alien lording it
over the younger men, to our great shame!

(*To Lycus.*)

Never shall you boast that I am your slave,
never will you reap the harvest of my work,
all I labored for. Go back whence you came;
rage there. So long as there is life in me,
you shall not kill the sons of Heracles.
He has not gone *so* deep beneath the earth.
Because you ruined, then usurped, this land,
he who gave it help must go without his due.
Am I a meddler, then, because I help
the friend who, being dead, needs help the most?
O right hand, how you ache to hold a spear,
but cannot, want foundering on weakness.
Else, I should have stopped your mouth that calls me slave,
and ruled this Thebes, in which you now exult,
with credit. But corrupt with evil schemes

and civil strife, this city lost its mind;
for were it sane, it would not live your slave.

Megara

Old sirs, I thank you. Friends rightly show
just indignation on their friends' behalf.
But do not let your rage on our account
involve your ruin too. Amphitryon,
hear what I think for what it may be worth.
I love my children. How not love these boys
born of my labors? I am in terror
of their death. And yet how base a thing it is
when a man will struggle with necessity!
We have to die. Then do we have to die
consumed alive, mocked by those we hate?—
for me a worse disaster than to die.
Our house and birth demand a better death.
Upon your helm the victor's glory sits,
forbidding that you die a coward's death;
while my husband needs no witnesses to swear
he would not want these sons of his to live
by living cowards. Because it hurts his sons,
disgraces break a man of noble birth;
and I must imitate my husband here.
Consider of what stuff your hopes are made;
you think your son will come from underground.
Who of all the dead comes home from Hades?
Or do you think you'll mellow *him* with prayers?
No, you must shun a brutal enemy;
yield to noble, understanding men
who, met halfway as friends, give mercy freely.
The thought had come to me that prayers might win
the children's banishment; but this is worse,
to preserve them for a life of beggary.
How does the saying go? Hardly one day
do men look kindly on their banished friend.

Dare death with us, which awaits you anyway.
By your great soul, I challenge you, old friend.
The man who sticks it out against his fate
shows spirit, but the spirit of a fool.
No man alive can budge necessity.

Chorus

I could have stopped the mouth of any man
who threatened you, had I my old strength back.
But now I am nothing. With you it rests,
Amphitryon, to avert disaster now.

Amphitryon

Not cowardice, not love of life, keep me
from death, but my hope to save these children.
I am in love, it seems, with what cannot be.

(*Turning to Lycus.*)

Here, king, here is my throat, ready for your sword;
murder me, stab me through, hurl me from a cliff,
but, I beg you, grant us both this one boon.
Murder us before you kill these children;
spare us from seeing that ghastly sight,
these boys gasping out their lives, crying
"Mother!" and "Grandfather!" For the rest,
do your worst. Our hope is gone; we have to die.

Megara

I beg you, grant me this one last request,
and so by one act you shall oblige us both.
Let me adorn my children for their death;
open those doors which are locked to us
and give them that much share of their father's house.

Lycus

I grant it. Attendants, undo the bolts!

(*Attendants slide open the center doors of the palace.*)

Go in and dress. I do not begrudge you clothes.
But when your dressing for your death is done,
then I shall give you to the world below.

(*Exit Lycus.*)

Megara

Come, my sons, follow your poor mother's steps
into your father's halls. Other men
possess his wealth; we still possess his name.

(*Exit Megara with children.*)

Amphitryon

For nothing, then, O Zeus, you shared my wife!
In vain we called you partner in my son!
Your love is even less than you pretended;
and I, mere man, am nobler than you, great god.
I did not betray the sons of Heracles.
You knew well enough to creep into my bed
and take what was not yours, what no man gave:
what do you know of saving those you love?
You are a callous god or were born unjust!

(*Exit Amphitryon to palace.*)

Chorus

STROPHE I

First for joy, the victor's song;
then the dirge; sing *ailinos* for Linos!
So Apollo sings, sweeping with golden pick
his lyre of lovely voice.
And so I sing of him
who went in darkness underground—
   let him be the son of Zeus,
   let him be Amphitryon's—
of him I sing, a dirge of praise,
a crown of song upon his labors.
For of noble deeds the praises are
   the glory of the dead.
First he cleared the grove of Zeus,

and slew the lion in its lair;
the tawny hide concealed his back,
oval of those awful jaws
   cowled his golden hair.

Antistrophe 1

Next the centaurs: slaughtered them,
that mountain-ranging savage race,
laid them low with poisoned shafts,
with winged arrows slew them all.
Too well the land had known them:
Peneios' lovely rapids,
vast plains, unharvested,
homesteads under Pelion,
and the places near Homole,
whence their cavalry rode forth
with weapons carved of pine,
   and tamed all Thessaly.
And next he slew the spotted hind
whose antlers grew of golden horn,
that robber-hind, that ravager,
whose horns now gild Oenoë's shrine,
   for Artemis the huntress.

Strophe 2

Then mounted to his car
and mastered with the bit
Diomedes' mares, that knew
no bridle, stabled in blood,
greedy jaws champing flesh,
foul mares that fed on men!
And thence crossed over
swirling silver, Hebros' waters,
on and on, performing labors
   for Mycenae's king.
And there by Pelion's headland,

near the waters of Anauros,
his shafts brought Cycnus down,
that stranger-slaying monster,
   host of Amphanaia.

ANTISTROPHE 2

Thence among the singing maidens,
western halls' Hesperides.
Plucked among the metal leaves
the golden fruit, and slew
the orchard's dragon-guard
whose tail of amber coiled the trunk
untouchably. He passed below the sea
and set a calmness in the lives of men
   whose living is the oar.
Under bellied heaven next,
he put his hand as prop:
there in the halls of Atlas,
his manliness held up
   heaven's starry halls.

STROPHE 3

He passed the swelling sea of black,
and fought the Amazonian force
foregathered at Maeotis
where the many rivers meet.
What town of Hellas missed him
as he mustered friends to fight,
to win the warrior women's
gold-encrusted robes, in quest
for a girdle's deadly quarry?
And Hellas won the prize, spoils
of a famous foreign queen,
   which now Mycenae keeps.
He seared each deadly hydra-head
of Lerna's thousand-headed hound;

in her venom dipped the shaft
that brought three-bodied Geryon down,
   herdsman of Erytheia.

Antistrophe 3

And many races more he ran,
and won in all the victor's crown,
whose harbor now is Hades' tears,
the final labor of them all;
there his life is disembarked
in grief. He comes no more.
His friends have left his house,
and Charon's ferry waits
to take his children's lives
the godless, lawless trip of no return.
To your hands your house still turns,
   and you are gone!
Could I have my youth once more,
could I shake my spear once more
beside the comrades of my youth,
my courage now would champion
your sons. But youth comes back no more
   that blessed me once.

Epode

Look: I see the children coming now,
wearing the garments of the grave,
sons of Heracles who once was great;
and there, his wife, drawing her sons
behind her as she comes; and the old man,
father of Heracles. O pitiful sight!
I cannot hold the tears that break
   from these old eyes.

(Enter Megara from the palace. She is followed by the children, dressed in the garments of the dead. Last comes Amphitryon.)

Megara

Where is the priest with sacrificial knife?
Where is the killer of our wretched lives?
Here the victims stand, ready for Hades.
O my boys, this incongruity of death:
beneath one yoke, old man, children and mother.
How miserably we die, these children and I!
Upon these faces now I look my last.
I gave you birth and brought you up to be
but mocked and murdered by our enemies.
  How bitterly my hopes for you have failed,
those hopes I founded on your father's words.

(*She turns to each child in turn.*)

To *you* your father would have left all Argos:
in Eurystheus' halls you would have ruled
and held the sway over rich Pelasgia.
It was upon your head he sometimes threw
the skin of tawny lion that he wore.
You, made king of chariot-loving Thebes,
would have inherited your mother's lands,
because you teased them from your father once.
Sometimes in play, he put in your right hand
that carven club he kept for self-defense.
To *you*, he would have left Oechalia,
ravaged once by his far-shooting shafts.
There are three of you, and with three kingdoms
your heroic father would have raised you up.
And I had chosen each of you a bride,
from Athens, Thebes, and Sparta, binding our house
by marriage, that having such strong anchors down,
you might in happiness ride out your lives.
Now all is gone, and fortune, veering round,
gives each of you your death as though a bride,
and in my tears your bridal shower is,
while your father's father mourns the feast

that makes you all the sons-in-law of death.
Which shall I take first, which of you the last,
to lift you up, take in my arms and kiss?
If only I could gather up my tears,
and like the tawny bee from every flower,
distil to one small nectar all my grief!
O dearest Heracles, if any voice
from here reaches to Hades, hear me now!
Your sons, your father, are dying . . . and I,
who was once called blessed because of you.
Help us, come! Come, even as a ghost;
even as a dream, your coming would suffice.
For these are cowards who destroy your sons.

Amphitryon

Send your prayers, my child, to the world below,
while I hold out my hands to heaven.
We implore you, Zeus, if still you mean to help,
help us now before it is too late.
How often have I called! In vain, my labors.
For death is on us like necessity.
  Our lives, old friends, are but a little while,
so let them run as sweetly as you can,
and give no thought to grief from day to day.
For time is not concerned to keep our hopes,
but hurries on its business, and is gone.
You see in me a man who once had fame,
who did great deeds; but fortune in one day
has snatched it from me as though a feather.
Great wealth, great reputation! I know no man
with whom they stay. Friends of my youth, farewell.
You look your last on him who loved you well.

(*Megara suddenly catches sight of Heracles approaching from a distance.*)

Megara

Look, Father! My dearest! Can it be?

Amphitryon

I cannot say. I dare not say, my child.

Megara

It *is* he, whom we heard was under earth,
unless some dream comes walking in the light.
A dream? This is no dream my longing makes!
It is *he*, Father, your son, no other!
Run, children, fasten to your father's robes
and never let him go! Quick, run! He comes
to rescue us and Zeus comes with him.

(Enter Heracles, armed with bow and arrows, his club in in his hand. He does not see his family at first, but salutes his halls.)

Heracles

I greet my hearth! I hail my house and halls!
How gladly I behold the light once more
and look on you!

(He sees his family.)

What is this I see?
my children before the house? with garlands
on their heads? and my wife surrounded
by a crowd of men? my father in tears?
What misfortune makes him cry? I'll go and ask
what disaster now has come upon my house.

Megara

O my dearest. . . .

Amphitryon

O daylight returning!

Megara

You come, alive, in time to rescue us!

Heracles

Father, what has happened? What does this mean?

Megara

Murder. Forgive me, Father, if I snatch
and speak the words that you should rightly say.
I am a woman: anguish hurts me more,
and my children were being put to death. . . .

Heracles

Apollo! what a prelude to your tale!

Megara

My father is dead. My brothers are dead.

Heracles

What! How did they die? Who killed them?

Megara

Murdered by Lycus, the upstart tyrant.

Heracles

In revolution? Or civil war?

Megara

Civil war. Now he rules our seven gates.

Heracles

But why should you and my father be afraid?

Megara

He planned to kill us: your sons, father, and me.

Heracles

What had he to fear from my orphaned sons?

Megara

Lest they take revenge some day for Creon's death.

Heracles

But why these garments? Why are they dressed for death?

Megara

It was for our own deaths we put them on.

Heracles

You would have died by violence? O gods!

Megara

We had no friends. We heard that you were dead.

Heracles

How did you come to give up hope for me?

Megara

The heralds of Eurystheus proclaimed you dead.

Heracles

Why did you abandon my house and hearth?

Megara

By force. He dragged your father from his bed.

Heracles

He had no shame, but so dishonored age?

Megara

Lycus have shame? He knows no such goddess.

Heracles

And were my friends so scarce when I was gone?

Megara

In misfortune, what friend remains a friend?

Heracles

They thought so little of my Minyan wars?

Megara

Again I say, misfortune has no friends.

Heracles

Rip from your heads those wreaths of Hades!
Lift your faces to the light; with seeing eyes,
take your sweet reprieve from death and darkness.
And I—a task for my one hand alone—

shall go and raze this upstart tyrant's house,
cut off that blaspheming head and give it
to the dogs to paw. All those men of Thebes
who took my goodness and returned me ill—
this bow with which I won the victor's crown
shall slaughter them with rain of wingèd shafts
till all Ismenus chokes upon the corpses
and Dirce's silver waters run with blood.
What should I defend if not my wife and sons
and my old father? Farewell, my labors!
for wrongly I preferred you more than these.
They would have died for me, and I should die
in their defense. Or is this bravery,
to do Eurystheus' orders and contend
with lions and hydras, and not to struggle
for my children's lives? From this time forth,
call me no more "Heracles the victor."

Chorus

This is right, that a man defend his sons,
his aged father, and his wedded wife.

Amphitryon

My son, it is like you to love your friends
and hate your foe. But do not act too fast.

Heracles

How do I act faster than I should?

Amphitryon

The king has henchmen, a mob of needy men
who pass themselves off for men of wealth.
These men, their substance drained away by sloth
and spending, have promoted civil strife
and wrecked the state to mulct their neighbors.
You were seen coming here. Beware therefore
lest your enemy be stronger than you guess.

Heracles

I do not care if all the city saw me!
But seeing a bird in some foreboding place,
I guessed some trouble had fallen on my house,
and thus forewarned, I entered secretly.

Amphitryon

Good. Go now, enter your house and greet your hearth.
Look on your father's house; let it behold you.
Shortly the king will come to hale us off
and slaughter us: your wife, your sons, and me.
Wait here, and everything shall come to hand;
with safety too. But let the city go,
my son, until we finish matters here.

Heracles

You advise me well. I will go within.
I owe first greetings to my household gods
because they brought me home from sunless caves
of Kore and Hades. I shall not slight them.

Amphitryon

Did you really descend to Hades, son?

Heracles

Yes; I brought back the triple-headed dog.

Amphitryon

You subdued him? or was he the goddess' gift?

Heracles

Subdued him. Luck was mine: I saw the mysteries.

Amphitryon

And is the monster at Eurystheus' house?

Heracles

No, at Hermione, in Demeter's grove.

Amphitryon

Does Eurystheus know of your return above?

Heracles

No, I came here first to learn of you.

Amphitryon

Why did you delay so long underground?

Heracles

To save Theseus from Hades, Father.

Amphitryon

Where is he now? Gone to his native land?

Heracles

He went to Athens, rejoicing to be free.

(*He turns and addresses his children.*)

Follow your father to the house, my sons,
for this, your going in, shall be more fair
than your coming out. Put your fears away,
and stop those tears that well up in your eyes.
And you, dear wife, gather your courage up,
tremble no more, and let my garments go.
I have no wings to fly from those I love.
Look:
They will not let me go, but clutch my clothes
more tightly. How close you came to death!

(*He sets down his bow and club and takes his children by the hands.*)

Here, I'll take your hands and lead you in my wake, POLITICAL IDEAS?
like a ship that tows its little boats behind,
for I accept this care and service
of my sons. Here all mankind is equal:
rich and poor alike, they love their children.
With wealth distinctions come: some possess it,
some do not. All mankind loves its children.

(*Exit Heracles with the children, followed by Megara and Amphitryon.*)

Chorus

STROPHE 1

Youth I long for always.
But old age lies on my head,
a weight more heavy than Aetna's rocks;
darkness hides
the light of my eyes.
Had I the wealth of an Asian king,
or a palace crammed with gold,
both would I give for youth,
loveliest in wealth,
in poverty, loveliest.
But old age I loathe: ugly,
murderous. Let the waves take it
so it comes no more to the homes
and cities of men! Let the wind
whirl it away forever!

ANTISTROPHE 1

If the gods were wise and understood
what human wisdom understands,
second youth would be their gift,
to seal the goodness of a man.
And so, conspicuous of life,
the good would run their race to death
and double back to light again.
But evil men should live their lap,
one single life, and run no more.
By such a sign all men would know
the wicked from the good,
as when the clouds are broken
and the sailor sees the stars.
But now the gods have put
between the noble and the base
no clear distinction down.
And time and age go wheeling on,
exalting only wealth.

STROPHE 2

Never shall I cease from this,
Muses with the Graces joining,
loveliness in yoke together.
I may not live without the Muses.
Let my head be always crowned!
May my old age always sing
of Memory, the Muses' mother,
always shall I sing the crown
of Heracles the victor!
So long as these remain—
  Dionysus' gift of wine,
  the lyre of seven strings
  the shrilling of the flute—
never shall I cease to sing,
  Muses who made me dance!

ANTISTROPHE 2

Paeans sing the Delian maidens,
a song for Leto's lovely son,
wheeling at the temple gates
the lovely mazes of the dance.
So paeans at your gate I raise,
pouring like the dying swan,
from hoary throat a song of praise.
I have a noble theme of song:
  He is the son of Zeus!
  But far beyond his birth,
  his courage lifts him up,
whose labors gave this mortal calm,
  who cleared away the beasts.

(*Enter Lycus, with attendants. Amphitryon emerges from the palace.*)

Lycus

None too soon, Amphitryon, have you appeared.
A long time now you've spent in dallying

with your robes and ornaments of death.
Go, call the wife and sons of Heracles
and bid them show themselves before the house.
On those terms, I let you clothe yourselves for death.

Amphitryon

King, you persecute in me a wretched man,
and by abusing us, you wrong the dead.
King you may be, but tread more gently here.
Death is your decree, and we accept it
as we must. As you decide, then so must we.

Lycus

Where is Megara? Where are the children?

Amphitryon

To chance a guess from here outside, I think . . .

Lycus

Well, what do you think? What makes you think so?

Amphitryon

. . . kneels at the hearth and makes her prayers . . .

Lycus

If she asks for life, her prayers are pointless.

Amphitryon

. . . and implores in vain her husband to come.

Lycus

He is not here to help. He will not come.

Amphitryon

Not unless some god restore him to us.

Lycus

Go inside and fetch her from the house.

Amphitryon

Then I should be accomplice in her death.

Lycus

Very well then. Since your scruples forbid,
I, who lack such petty fears, shall go and fetch
the mother and her sons. Attend me, guards,
and help me put good riddance to this chore.

(*Exit Lycus, attended by guards, into the palace.*)

Amphitryon

Go, march in to your fate. Someone, I think,
will see you in. Expect for what you did
evil in return. How justly, old friends,
into that net whose meshes hide the sword,
he goes, the man who would have slaughtered us,
coward that he is! I'll go in and watch
his body fall. This is sweet: to see your foe
perish and pay to justice all he owes.

(*Exit Amphitryon into the palace.*)

STROPHE 1

Chorus

Disaster is reversed!
The tyrant's life turns back to Hades!
Justice flows back! O fate of the gods,
returning!

Your time has come. You go now where the price
for outrage on your betters must be paid.

Joy once more! Overboard with grief!
The king has come again!
He has come, of whom I had no hope,
my country's king, come back again!

Peer within the house, old friends. Let me see
if what I hope to see is taking place.

Lycus

(*Within.*)

Help! Help!

Chorus

ANTISTROPHE 1

From within the song begins
I long to hear. That cry
was prelude to his death:
the tyrant's death is near.

Lycus

O land of Cadmus! Treachery! I die!

Chorus

Die: you would have killed. Show your boldness now
as you repay to justice all you owe.

What lying mortal made that fable
that mindless tale
that slander on the blessed?
Who denied the gods are strong?

Old friends, the godless man is dead!
The house is silent. Turn to the dances!
Those I love now prosper as I hoped.

STROPHE 2

Let dance and feasting now prevail
throughout this holy town of Thebes!
Joy and mourning change their places,
old disaster turns to dancing!
Change now rings my change of song!
The new king runs to death, the old king rules!
Our king runs home from Hades' harbor!
He comes again, he comes, my king and hope,
of whom my hope despaired.

ANTISTROPHE 2

The gods of heaven do prevail:
they raise the good and scourge the bad.
Excess of happiness—it drives
men's minds awry; in its train

comes on corrupted power.
No man foresees the final stretch of time.
Evil lures him, justice races by,
until he wrecks at last the somber car
  that holds his happiness.

STROPHE 3

O Ismenus, come with crowns!
Dance and sing: you gleaming streets
of seven-gated Thebes!
Come, O Dirce, lovely river,
leave your father's waters, bring
the nymphs, Asopus' daughters!
Come and sing the famous crown
of Heracles the victor!
O wooded crag of Delphi,
O Muses' homes on Helicon!
make my city's walls resound,
echo back the joy of Thebes,
city where the sown men rose
with shields of bronze, where still
their children's children dwell,
  a blessed light to Thebes!

ANTISTROPHE 3

O marriage-bed two bridegrooms shared!
One was man; the other, Zeus,
who entered in the bridal bed
and with Alcmene lay.
How true, O Zeus, that marriage
proves to be! Your part therein,
against all doubt, is proven true!
For time at last has clearly shown the strength
of Heracles the hero.
He made his way from Pluto's halls;
he left the dungeon underground.

He is to me a better king
than that ignoble lord:
comparison made plain
in the struggle of the sword,
if justice still finds favor
among the blessed gods.

(A crash of thunder. The figure of Madness, gorgon-faced and holding a goad, appears in a black chariot on the roof of the palace. On the other side of the roof Iris is seen.)

Ah! Ah!
Is the same terror on us all?
Look, old friends: what phantom hovers on the house?

Fly, fly!
Stir your heavy limbs! Back, away!

Lord Paian, help us! Avert disaster!

Iris

Courage, old men. You see there, Madness,
child of night, and me, servant of the gods,
Iris. We bring no harm upon your city.
Against one man alone our war is waged,
him whom men call Alcmene's son by Zeus.
Until his bitter labors had been done,
his fate preserved him; nor would father Zeus
let me or Hera do him any harm.
But now Eurystheus' orders have been done,
Hera plans, by making him destroy his sons,
to taint him with fresh murder; and I agree.
Up, then, unmarried child of blackest Night,
rouse up, harden that relentless heart,
send madness on this man, confound his mind
and make him kill his sons. Madden his feet;
drive him, goad him, shake out the sails of death
and speed his passage over Acheron,
where he must take his crown of lovely sons.
Let him learn what Hera's anger is,

and what is mine. For the gods are nothing,
and men prevail, if this one man escape.

Madness

I was born of noble birth: my mother
is the Night, and my father, Uranus.
My functions make me loathsome to the gods,
nor do I gladly visit men I love.
And I advise both you and Hera now,
lest I see you stumble, to hear me out.
This man against whose house you drive me on
has won great fame on earth and with the gods.
He reclaimed the pathless earth and raging sea,
and he alone held up the honors of the gods
when they wilted at the hands of evil men.
I advise you: renounce these wicked plans.

Iris

Hera's scheme and mine need no advice from you.

Madness

I would place you on the better path: you choose the worse.

Iris

Hera has not sent you down to show your sanity.

Madness

O Sun, be my witness: I act against my will.
But since I must perform the service you and Hera ask,
in full cry, like the hound that bays the huntsman,
go I will: to the heart of Heracles I run,
more fast, more wild than ocean's groaning breakers go,
than earthquake, or the thunder's agonizing crack!
I shall batter through the roof and leap upon the house!
He shall kill his sons and, killing, shall not know
he kills what he begot, until my madness leave him.
Look: already, head writhing, he leaps the starting-post;
jumps and now stops; his eyeballs bulge, and pupils roll;

his breath comes heaving up, a bull about to charge!
And now he bellows up the horrid fates from hell;
he groans and shouts; he dances to the pipes of terror!
Soar to Olympus, Iris, on your honored way,
while I now sink, unseen, to the house of Heracles.

(Iris and Madness disappear. As they go, a weird piping of the flute begins, now soft, now loud, broken in rhythm, pitched insanely, and then suddenly still.)

Chorus

O city, mourn! Your flower
is cut down, the son of Zeus.
O Hellas, mourn! You have lost
your savior! He dances now
to the fatal flutes of madness!

Madness has mounted her car;
she goads her team!
she drives for death!
O gorgon of Night, O hiss
of a hundred snakes! O Madness,
whose look makes stones of men!

Instantly, god's fortune is reversed!
Instantly, and father murders sons!

Amphitryon

O horror!

(Within.)

Chorus

O Zeus, your son has lost his sons!
Vengeance, mad, implacable, exacts
the penalty! Disaster lays him low!

Amphitryon

O my house!

Chorus

Now the dance begins! Not here,
the drums! no lovely thyrsos here!

Amphitryon
O my home!

Chorus
For blood, she drives, for blood!
No wine of Dionysus here!

Amphitryon
Fly, children, save yourselves!

Chorus
Horrid,
horrid piping of the flute!
His sons, he hunts them down!
Madness through the house,
madness dancing death!

Amphitryon
O grief!

Chorus
I grieve for those two,
for the old man, for the mother
who bore, who nursed her sons in vain!

Look, look!
Whirlwind shakes the house, the roof falls!

Ah! on the roof!
O daughter of Zeus, what do you do?
You have brought upon this house
ruin that reaches to hell,
as once you ruined Enceladus!

(*A messenger appears from the palace.*)

Messenger
O bodies blanched with age. . . .

Chorus
Why that cry?

Messenger
Horror in the house!

Chorus

O my prophetic fears!

Messenger

The children live no more.

Chorus

Ah. . . .

Messenger

Mourn them, grieve them.

Chorus

Cruel murder,
O cruel hands of a father!

Messenger

No words could tell what we have seen.

Chorus

How did it happen, how this madness,
children killed by a father's hands?
How did disaster strike, madness
hurled from heaven on this house?
How did those pitiful children die?

Messenger

Offerings to Zeus were set before the hearth
to purify the house, for Heracles
had cast the body of the king outside.
There the children stood, in lovely cluster,
with Megara and the old man. In holy hush
the basket made the circle of the hearth.
And then, as Heracles reached out his hand
to take the torch and dip it in the water,
he stood stockstill. There he stood, not moving,
while the children stared. Suddenly he changed:
his eyes rolled and bulged from their sockets,
and the veins stood out, gorged with blood, and froth
began to trickle down his bearded chin.

Then he spoke, laughing like a maniac:
"Why hallow fire, Father, to cleanse the house
before I kill Eurystheus? Why double work,
when at one blow I might complete my task?
I'll go and fetch Eurystheus' head, add it
to that other corpse, then purify my hands.
Empty your water out! Drop those baskets!
Someone fetch my bow. Put weapons in my hands:
I march against Mycenae! Let me have
crowbars and picks: the Cyclopes built well,
cramping stone on stone with plumb and mallet,
but with my pick I'll rip them down again."
Then he fancied that his chariot stood there;
he made as though to leap its rails, and rode off,
prodding with his hand as though it held a goad.
Whether to laugh or shudder, we could not tell.
We stared at one another. Then one man asked,
"Is the master playing, or is he . . . mad?"
Up and down, throughout the house, he drove,
and riding through the great hall, claimed it was
Nisus' city, though it was, in fact, his house.
He threw himself to the floor, and acted out
a feast. He tarried there a while, then said
he was approaching Isthmus' wooded valley.
He unstrapped his buckles and stripped himself bare,
and wrestled with no one; then called for silence
and crowned himself the victor of a match
that never was. Then raged against Eurystheus,
and said he'd come to Mycenae. His father
caught him by that muscled hand and said:
"What do you mean, my son? What is this journey
that you make? Or has the blood of those you've slain
made you mad?" He thought Eurystheus' father
had come, trembling, to supplicate his hand;
pushed him away, and set his bow and arrows
against his sons. He thought he was killing

Eurystheus' children. Trembling with terror,
they rushed here and there; one hid beneath
his mother's robes, one ran to the shadow
of a pillar, and the last crouched like a bird
below the altar. Their mother shrieked:
"You are their father! Will you kill your sons?"
And shouts broke from the old man and the slaves.
Around the pillar he pursued his son
in dreadful circles, then caught up with him
and pierced him to the heart. Backward he fell,
dying, and stained the flagstones with his blood.
His father shouted in triumph, exulting,
"Here is the first of Eurystheus' youngsters dead;
his death repays me for his father's hate."
He aimed his bow at the second, who crouched
below the altar's base, trying to hide.
The boy leaped first, fell at his father's knees
and held his hand up to his father's chin.
"Dearest Father," he cried, "do not murder me.
I am your own son, yours, not Eurystheus'!"
But he stared from stony gorgon eyes,
found his son too close to draw the bow,
and brought his club down on that golden head,
and smashed the skull, as though a blacksmith
smiting steel. Now that his second son lay dead,
he rushed to kill the single victim left.
But before he drew the bow, the mother
seized her child, ran within and locked the doors.
And, as though these were the Cyclopean walls,
he pried the panels up, ripped out the jambs,
and with one arrow brought down son and wife.
And then he rushed to kill his father too,
but look! a phantom came—or so it seemed to us—
Pallas, with plumed helm, brandishing a spear.
She hurled a rock; it struck him on the chest,
stopped short his murderous rage and knocked him

into sleep. He slumped to the floor and hit
his back against a pillar which had fallen there,
snapped in two pieces when the roof collapsed.
Delivered from the fear that made us run,
we helped the old man lash him down with ropes
against the pillar, lest when he awakes
still greater grief be added to the rest.
He sleeps now, wretched man, no happy sleep,
killer of his wife and sons. I do not know
one man alive more miserable than this.

(*Exit messenger.*)

Chorus

The hill of Argos had a murder once
Danaus' daughters did, murder's byword,
unbelievable in Hellas!
But murder here has far outrun,
surpassed by far
that ancient crime.

And Procne's noble son was slain,
murdered by his mother's hands and made,
I say, the Muses' sacrifice.
She had but that one son,
while you, poor wretch, had three,
all murdered by your madness.
What dirge, what song
shall I sing for the dead?
What dance shall I dance for death?

(*The great central doors of the palace slide slowly apart, revealing, in the center court, Heracles asleep, bound to a broken pillar. The bodies of Megara and the children beside him are wheeled on the stage in the eccyclema.*)

Ah, look!
Look: the great doors
of the palace slide apart!

Look there!
Look: the children's corpses

beside their wretched father.
How terribly he lies asleep
after his children's slaughter!

Ropes around his body,
knotted cords bind Heracles,
cables lash him down
to the pillars of his house.

Here the old man comes, dragging behind
with heavy steps, mourning in bitterness
like some bird whose unfledged covey is slain.

Amphitryon
Hush, old men of Cadmus' city,
and let him sleep. Hush:
let him forget his grief.

Chorus
I weep for you, old friend,
for these boys, and for that head
that wore the victor's crown.

Amphitryon
Stand further off: not a sound,
not a cry. His sleep is deep,
his sleep is calm. Let him lie.

Chorus
What murder . . .

Amphitryon
Hush! Be still: you add but grief.

Chorus
. . . poured out, piled high!

Amphitryon
Softly, gently, old friends. Mourn
in quiet: not a word, not a cry.
If he awakes and breaks his bonds,

he will destroy us all:
father, city, and his house.

Chorus

I cannot hold my grief.

Amphitryon

Hush:
let me hear his breathing.

Chorus

Does he sleep?

Amphitryon

He sleeps, but sleeps
as dead men do, because he slew his wife
and killed his sons with twanging bow.

Chorus

Grieve then, mourn!

Amphitryon

I mourn, I grieve.

Chorus

Mourn for these dead children.

Amphitryon

Ah. . . .

Chorus

Mourn your son, grieve for him.

Amphitryon

Ah. . . .

Chorus

Old friend. . . .

Amphitryon

Hush, be still:
he stirs and turns! He wakes! Quick,
let me hide myself in darkness here.

Chrous

Courage: darkness lies upon his eyes.

Amphitryon

Take care, take care. My grief is such,
I have no fear to leave the light and die.
But if he murders me who begot him,
he shall add a greater grief to these,
and have on him the curse of father's blood.

Chorus

Best for you it would have been
if you had died that very day
you took revenge on those who slew
the kinsmen of your wife, the day
you sacked the city of the Taphians!

Amphitryon

Run, run, old friends, back from the house,
away! He wakes! Run, run
from his reawakened rage!
He wakes to pile murder on murder,
to dance madness through all Thebes!

Chorus

O Zeus, why have you hated him so much,
your own son? Why launched him on this sea of grief?

Heracles

How now?
I do breathe . . . what I ought to see, I see:
heaven and earth, the gleaming shafts of the sun. . . .
But how strangely my muddled senses swim,
as on a choppy sea . . . my breath comes warm,
torn up unsteadily from heaving lungs. . . .
And look: I sit here, like a ship lashed tight
with cables binding my chest and arms,
moored to a piece of broken masonry;
and there, close beside me, corpses lie . . .

and my bow and arrows littered on the ground,
those faithful former comrades of my arms,
that guarded my chest, and I guarded them.
Have I come back to Hades? Have I run
Eurystheus' race again? Hades? But how?
No, for I see no rock of Sisyphus,
no Pluto, no queen Demeter's sceptre.
I am bewildered. Where could *I* be helpless?
Help! Is there some friend of mine, near or far,
who could help me in my bewilderment?
For all I took for granted now seems strange. . . .

Amphitryon
Old friends, shall I approach my affliction?

Chorus
Go, and I'll go with you, sharing in your grief.

Heracles
Why do you cry, Father, and hide your eyes?
Why do you stand off from the son you love?

Amphitryon
O my son, *my* son, whatever you have done. . . .

Heracles
What have I done that you should weep for it?

Amphitryon
Even a god would weep, if he knew it.

Heracles
A great grief it must be; but you hide it.

Amphitryon
It is there to see, if you could but see it.

Heracles
Tell me if you mean my life is not the same.

Amphitryon
Tell me if you are sane; then I shall speak.

Heracles

O gods, how ominous these questions are!

Amphitryon

I wonder even now if you are not mad. . . .

Heracles

Mad? I cannot remember being mad.

Amphitryon

Friends, shall I loose his ropes? What should I do?

Heracles

Tell me who bound me! Who disgraced me so?

Amphitryon

Your troubles are enough. Let the others go.

Heracles

I say no more. Will you tell me now?

Amphitryon

O Zeus, do you see these deeds Hera has done?

Heracles

Is it from *her* hate our sufferings come?

Amphitryon

Let the goddess go. Shoulder your own grief.

Heracles

I am ruined. Your words will be disaster.

(*Amphitryon removes the shrouds from the children's corpses.*)

Amphitryon

Look. Look at the bodies of your children.

Heracles

Oh horrible! What awful sight is this?

Amphitryon

Your unnatural war against your sons.

Heracles
War? What war do you mean? Who killed these boys?

Amphitryon
You and your bow and some god are all guilty.

Heracles
What! I did it? O Father, herald of evil!

Amphitryon
You were mad. Your questions asked for grief.

Heracles
And it was I who murdered wife as well?

Amphitryon
All this was the work of your hand alone.

Heracles
O black night of grief which covers me!

Amphitryon
It was because of that you saw me weep.

Heracles
Did I ruin all my house in my madness?

Amphitryon
I know but this: everything you have is grief.

Heracles
Where did my madness take me? Where did I die?

Amphitryon
By the altar, as you purified your hands.

Heracles
Why then am I so sparing of this life,
born the killer of my dearest sons?
Let me avenge my children's murder:
let me hurl myself down from some sheer rock,
or drive the whetted sword against my side,

or expunge with fire this body's madness
and burn away this guilt which sticks to my life!

(*He glances to the right and sees Theseus approaching.*)

But look: Theseus comes, my friend and kinsman,
intruding on my strategies for death.
And seeing me, the taint of murdered sons
shall enter at the eye of my dearest friend.
What shall I do? Where can this shame be hid?
Oh for wings to fly! to plunge beneath the earth!
Here: let my garments hide my head in darkness,
in shame, in horror of this deed I did,
and so concealed, I'll shelter him from harm,
and keep pollution from the innocent.

(*Enter Theseus, unattended.*)

Theseus

I come, old man, leading the youth of Athens,
bringing alliance to your son; my men
wait under arms by the stream of Asopos.
A rumor came to Erechtheus' city
that Lycus had seized the sceptre of this land
and was engaged in war against your house.
And so, in gratitude to Heracles
who saved me from Hades, I have come,
old man, if you should need a helping hand.

(*He sees the corpses of the children.*)

Ah!
What bodies are these scattered on the ground?
Have I arrived too late, preceded here
by some disaster? Who killed these boys?
That woman lying there, whose wife was she?
Children are not mustered on the field of war:
no, this is some newer sorrow I find here.

Amphitryon

O lord of the olive-bearing hill. . . .

Theseus
Why do you speak in those heavy tones of grief?

Amphitryon
See what grief the gods have given.

Theseus
Whose children are these over whom you mourn?

Amphitryon
O gods, my son begot these boys,
begot them, killed them, his own blood.

Theseus
Unsay those words!

Amphitryon
Would that I could!

Theseus
Oh horrible tale!

Amphitryon
We are ruined and lost.

Theseus
How did it happen? Tell me how.

Amphitryon
Dead in the blow of madness,
by arrows dipped in the blood
of the hundred-headed hydra. . . .

Theseus
This is Hera's war. Who lies there by the bodies?

Amphitryon
My son, my most unhappy son,
who fought with giant-killing spear
beside the gods at Phlegraia.

Theseus
What mortal man was ever cursed like this?

Amphitryon

Among all men you would not find,
greater wretchedness, greater suffering
than this.

Theseus

Why does he hide his head beneath his robes?

Amphitryon

Shame of meeting your eye,
shame before friends and kin,
shame for his murdered sons.

Theseus

I come to share his grief. Uncover him.

Amphitryon

My son, drop your robe from your eyes,
show your forehead to the sun.
A friend has come, a rival weight
to counterpoise your grief.
O my son, I impore you,
by your beard, your knees, your hand,
by an old man's tears:
tame that lion of your rage
that roars you on to death,
yoking grief to grief.

Theseus

I call on you, huddled there in misery:
lift up your head and show your face to friends.
There is no cloud whose utter blackness
could conceal in night a sorrow like yours.
Why wave me off, warning me of blood?
Are you afraid mere words would pollute me?
What do I care if your misfortunes fall
on me? You were my good fortune once:
you saved me from the dead, brought me back to light.
I loathe a friend whose gratitude grows old,

a friend who takes his friend's prosperity
but will not voyage with him in his grief.
Rise up; uncover that afflicted head
and look on us. This is courage in a man:
to bear unflinchingly what heaven sends.

(*He raises Heracles to his feet and uncovers his head.*)

Heracles
Theseus, have you seen this field of fallen sons?

Theseus
I heard. I see the grief to which you point.

Heracles
How could you then uncloak me to the sun?

Theseus
No mortal man can stain what is divine.

Heracles
Away, rash friend! Flee my foul pollution.

Theseus
Where there is love contagion cannot come.

Heracles
I thank you. How right I was to help you once.

Theseus
You saved me then, and now I pity you.

Heracles
A man to be pitied: I slew my children.

Theseus
My tears, my gratitude, I mourn your grief.

Heracles
Have you ever seen more misery than this?

Theseus
Your wretchedness towers up and touches heaven.

Heracles
Then where it touches heaven, I shall strike.

Theseus
What do you think the gods care for your threats?

Heracles
Heaven is proud. And I am proud to heaven.

Theseus
No more: your presumption will be punished.

Heracles
My hold is full: there is no room for more.

Theseus
What will you do? Where does your passion run?

Heracles
To death: to go back whence I came, beneath the earth.

Theseus
These are the words of an ordinary man.

Heracles
Will you, who did not suffer, preach to me?

Theseus
Is this that Heracles who endured so much?

Heracles
Not *so* much. Endurance has an end.

Theseus
Mankind's benefactor, man's greatest friend?

Heracles
What good are men to me? Hera rules.

Theseus
You die so mean a death? Hellas forbids it.

Heracles

Listen: let me tell you what makes a mock
at your advice. Let me show you my life:
a life not worth living now, or ever.
Take my father first, a man who killed
my mother's father and having such a curse,
married Alcmene who gave birth to me.
When a house is built on poor foundations,
then its descendants are the heirs of grief.
Then Zeus—whoever Zeus may be—begot me
for Hera's hatred. Take no offense, old man,
for I count you my father now, not Zeus.
While I was still at suck, she set her snakes
with gorgon eyes to slither in my crib
and strangle me. And when I grew older
and a belt of muscle bound my body—
why recite all those labors I endured?
All those wars I fought, those beasts I slew,
those lions and triple-bodied Typhons,
giants, and four-legged Centaur hordes!
I killed the hydra, that hound whose heads
grew back as soon as lopped. My countless labors done,
I descended down among the sullen dead
to do Eurystheus' bidding and bring to light
the triple-headed hound who guards the gates of hell.
And now my last worst labor has been done:
I slew my children and crowned my house with grief.
And this is how I stand: I cannot stay
with those I love at Thebes. If I remain,
what temple, what assembly of my friends
will have me? My curse is unapproachable.
Go to Argos then? No, I am banished there.
Settle in some other city then,
where notoriety shall pick me out
to be watched and goaded by bitter gibes—
"Is this the son of Zeus, who killed his wife

and sons? Away with him! Let him die elsewhere."
[To a man who prospers and is blessed,
all change is grief; but the man who lives
akin to trouble minds disaster less.]
But to this pitch of grief my life has come:
the earth itself will groan, forbidding me
to touch the ground, rivers and seas cry out
against my crossing-over, and I am
like Ixion, bound forever to a wheel.
This is the best, that I be seen no more
in Hellas, where I prospered and was great.
Why should I live? What profit have I,
having a life both useless and accursed?
Let the noble wife of Zeus begin the dance,
pounding with her feet Olympus' gleaming floors!
For she accomplished what her heart desired,
and hurled the greatest man of Hellas down
in utter ruin. Who could offer prayers
to such a goddess? Jealous of Zeus
for a mortal woman's sake, she has destroyed
Hellas' greatest friend, though he was guiltless.

Theseus

No other god is implicated here,
except the wife of Zeus. Rightly you judge.
My advice is this: be patient, suffer
what you must, and do not yield to grief.
Fate exempts no man; all men are flawed,
and so the gods, unless the poets lie.
Do not the gods commit adultery?
Have they not cast their fathers into chains,
in pursuit of power? Yet all the same,
despite their crimes, they live upon Olympos.
How dare you then, mortal that you are,
to protest your fate, when the gods do not?
Obey the law and leave your native Thebes

and follow after me to Pallas' city.
There I shall purify your hands of blood,
give you a home and a share of my wealth.
All those gifts I have because I killed
the Minotaur and saved twice seven youths,
I cede to you. Everywhere throughout my land,
plots of earth have been reserved for me.
These I now assign to you, to bear your name
until you die. And when you go to Hades,
Athens shall raise you up a monument
of stone, and honor you with sacrifice.
And so my city, helping a noble man,
shall win from Hellas a lovely crown of fame.
This thanks and this return I make you now,
who saved me once. For now you need a friend.
[He needs no friends who has the love of gods.
For when god helps a man, he has help enough.]

Heracles

Ah, all this has no bearing on my grief;
but I do not believe the gods commit
adultery, or bind each other in chains.
I never did believe it; I never shall;
nor that one god is tyrant of the rest.
If god is truly god, he is perfect,
lacking nothing. These are poets' wretched lies.
Even in my misery I asked myself,
would it not be cowardice to die?
The man who cannot bear up under fate
could never face the weapons of a man
I shall prevail against death. I shall go
to your city. I accept your countless gifts.
For countless were the labors I endured;
never yet have I refused, never yet
have I wept, and never did I think

that I should come to this: tears in my eyes.
But now, I see, I must serve necessity.
  And now you see me banished, old man;
you see in me the killer of my sons.
Give them to the grave, give them the tribute
of your tears, for the law forbids me this.
Let them lie there in their mother's arms,
united in their grief, as they were then,
before, in ignorance, I killed them all.
And when the earth conceals their small remains,
live on in this city here, and though it hurt,
compel your soul to bear misfortune with me.
  O my sons, the father who gave you life
has slain you all, and never shall you reap
that harvest of my life, all I labored for,
that heritage of fame I toiled to leave you.
You too, poor wife, I killed: unkind return
for having kept the honor of my bed,
for all your weary vigil in my house.
  O wretched wife and sons! Wretched father!
In grief I now unyoke myself from you.
O bitter sweetness of this last embrace!

(*He turns from his final farewell to his wife and children and picks up his bow and arrows.*)

O my weapons, bitter partners of my life!
What shall I do? Let you go, or keep you,
knocking against my ribs and always saying,
"With us you murdered wife and sons. Wearing us,
you wear your children's killers." Can that be worn?
What could I reply? Yet, naked of these arms,
with which I did the greatest deeds in Hellas,
must I die in shame at my enemies' hands?
No, they must be borne; but in pain I bear them.
  Hold with me, Theseus, in one thing more.

Help me take to Argos the monstrous dog,
lest, alone and desolate of sons, I die.
O land of Cadmus, O people of Thebes,
mourn with me, grieve with me, attend my children
to the grave! And with one voice mourn us all,
the dead and me. For all of us have died,
all struck down by one blow of Hera's hate.

Theseus

Rise up, unfortunate friend. Have done with tears.

Heracles

I cannot rise. My limbs are rooted here.

Theseus

Then necessity breaks even the strong.

Heracles

Oh to be a stone! To feel no grief!

Theseus

Enough. Give your hand to your helping friend.

Heracles

Take care. I may pollute your clothes with blood.

Theseus

Pollute them then. Spare not. I do not care.

Heracles

My sons are dead; now you shall be my son.

Theseus

Place your hand on my shoulder. I shall lead you.

Heracles

A yoke of love, but one of us in grief.
O Father, choose a man like this for friend.

Amphitryon

The land that gave him birth has noble sons.

Heracles
Theseus, turn me back. Let me see my sons.

Theseus
Is this a remedy to ease your grief?

Heracles
I long for it, yearn to embrace my father.

Amphitryon
My arms are waiting. I too desire it.

Theseus
Have you forgotten your labors so far?

Heracles
All those labors I endured were less than these.

Theseus
If someone sees your weakness, he will not praise you.

Heracles
I live: am I so low? You did not think so once.

Theseus
Once, no. But where now is famous Heracles?

Heracles
What were you when you were underground?

Theseus
In courage I was the least of men.

Heracles
Then will you say my grief degrades me now?

Theseus
Forward!

Heracles
Farewell, father!

Amphitryon
Farewell, my son.

Heracles

Bury my children.

Amphitryon

Who will bury me?

Heracles

I.

Amphitryon

When will you come?

Heracles

When you bury them.

Amphitryon

How?

Heracles

I shall have them brought from Thebes to Athens.
Take my children out, take them to their graves,
while I, whose whole house has gone down in grief,
am towed in Theseus' wake like some little boat.
The man who would prefer great wealth or strength
more than love, more than friends, is diseased of soul.

REPETITION OF "IMAGE" FROM THE BEGINNING.

Chorus

We go in grief, we go in tears,
who lose in you our greatest friend.

(Theseus and Heracles leave by the left. The chorus goes to the right, while Amphitryon slowly follows the eccyclema with the bodies of Megara and the children inside the palace. The great doors close behind them.)

IPHIGENIA IN TAURIS

Translated by Witter Bynner
Introduced by Richmond Lattimore

INTRODUCTION TO *IPHIGENIA IN TAURIS*

The Date

THERE is no external evidence for the date of *Iphigenia in Tauris* (it should be *Iphigenia among the Taurians*, but the other title has become regular through use); it has, however, been generally placed between 414 and 410 B.C., and there are good reasons for this. Meter is an excellent guide in dating the plays of Euripides, and metrically this play is similar to *The Trojan Women* (415), *Electra* (413), and *Helen* (412). In structure and plot *Iphigenia* is a romance or romantic comedy, and Euripides at this time seems to have been much interested in the possibilities of this type of play. The plots of *Iphigenia* and *Helen* are in many ways almost identical. In both, a woman who has been miraculously transported to the barbaric ends of the earth (Scythia, Egypt) and there held in honorable captivity is convinced, on the slightest kind of evidence, that the man in the world she loves most (brother, husband), her sole possible deliverer, is dead. Almost immediately she meets this very man and, after some misunderstanding, rushes into his arms in a joyful recognition scene. She then, with female guile (women, to Euripides, are more strategic than men) contrives their escape by working on the simple piety of the barbarian king, whose vengefulness is dispelled by the appearance of divinities (Athene, the Heavenly Twins), and all end at peace in the prospect of a happy future. This similarity might, however, be less striking if we possessed the lost plays of Euripides, since it is clear that he wrote many romantic comedies. *Ion* (possibly 411 B.C.) shares some of these features (supposed death and miraculous transportation, catastrophe barely averted, climax in recognition, happy ending) but is an example of the purer foundling-story. Our tentative date also goes well with the fact that at the end of his career Euripides was much interested in exploring the ramifications of the saga of the House of Atreus

(*Electra*, 413; *Helen*, 412; *Orestes*, about 408; *Iphigenia at Aulis*, posthumous), though the plays do not connect with each other and often conflict in choice of legendary variants.

Iphigenia was probably not produced with *Electra* in 413, since Orestes appears in both plays but with rather different characteristics, and since the predictions at the end of *Electra* ignore the expedition to the Taurians; nor, probably, was it produced with *Helen* in 412, since the dramas are too much alike to have been given together. We must then choose between 414 and 411 (the style is not "late" enough for any posterior date); my own uncertain choice is 414.

The Play

Iphigenia in Tauris was of course presented as a tragedy, but it is not "tragical" like *Medea* or *Hippolytus*. The formulae by which we are accustomed to interpret tragedy—the tragic fault or tragic choice (*hamartia*), the punishment of *hybris* (whatever that means), the irreconcilable conflict of characters, or justified revenge breeding new hatred and wrong—do not apply here and can be blissfully ignored. Euripides is more interested in How than in Why, and even as romantic comedy *Iphigenia* is less seriously problematical, cuts less deep, than *Alcestis* or *Ion*. Note how briskly the murder of Clytemnestra is disposed of, lines 924–27.

But the cheerfulness is serious, and in it I find two dominant ideals. One is the love of Greece. Euripides has been sobered by the horrors of internecine war, and has dropped the narrow, often bellicose pro-Athenian theme, which appears in *Heracleidae* and *Andromache* and *The Suppliants*, in favor of a wider Hellenism. His homesick Greeks find no comfort in even the friendliness of outlanders and long for Greece, all Greece or any of Greece, not merely Athens. The other ideal is friendship, the devoted, disinterested friendship of Admetus, Heracles, and Apollo in *Alcestis*, of Heracles and Theseus in *Heracles*, of Orestes, Pylades, and Electra in *Orestes* (a trio of cutthroats, to be sure, but their love seems to be real), and of the three friends here. Friendship and the love of Greek for Greek may indeed be symbolized for Euripides during this period in those

Dorian twins, Castor and Polydeuces (Pollux) who appear at the end of *Helen* and *Electra*. Polydeuces refused to survive his brother. The twins have no place in this story; yet Euripides goes out of his way to bring them in (l. 272), since they are the prototypes and patrons of those who put all selfishness aside and make the fortunes of their friends their own.

The Translation

The editors asked the distinguished poet Witter Bynner for permission to use his translation originally made in 1915. This translation seemed to them to be in many ways the first modern translation. The present text represents Mr. Bynner's carefully polished revision of a manuscript created under circumstances best recounted by him:

It might be wondered, when what little Greek I had learned at college was forgotten, why and how I came to venture a version in English of a Euripidean play.

In 1914, Isadora Duncan with her six dancers had for some time been bringing Greek figures and friezes to life on the stages of several nations. Almost everyone connected in those days with any of the arts knew Isadora; and when she had been given use of the New Theater near Columbus Circle in New York, later called the Century Theater, we often heard her wish for a "right translation" of a Greek play to produce there. She had removed orchestra seats to make a deep-aproned stage on which she offered almost daily, as public performances, her rehearsals and experiments in dance and drama. Charging dearly for what lower seats were left but only ten cents for a gallery seat, she attracted substantial and ardent audiences to an exciting laboratory unique in American history. After her production of *Oedipus Rex*—the lead well played by her brother, Augustin—she kept begging me to try my hand at a version of *Iphigenia in Tauris*, which, she said from some knowledge or other, "though superbly simple in the original, had never been humanly translated into English, but always with stilted inversions and scholarly heaviness, and the sense subjected to the sound."

She made me try it, the choruses first. Scenes of the play were to follow and be combined into growing length for performance, as fast as I could write them. We had put on the stage all of the choruses, for Margherita Duncan and Helen Freeman, besides the six girls and herself, before someone discovered and reported that by living in the theater's large, luxurious dressing-rooms Isadora and her group were breaking New York's fire regulations. So the whole experiment ended. But I finished the play, which was published as a single volume in 1915 and again, as part of my *Book of Plays*, in 1922. Both times, forgetting that we had omitted certain sections of the choruses which Isadora had thought too remotely allusive to be understood or effective, I neglected to restore them for print. They are included, however, in the present volume. I must add that in making the text for Isadora I relied only on close study of all English versions available. In revising it through the past two years, I have kept the choruses more or less as they were, a sort of musical accompaniment to the drama, but have otherwise written and discarded some seven manuscripts, with the devoted intent that what I could do for it might become ever simpler, clearer, and worthier of the humanist who wrote it.

For general accuracy, this new version has had the supervision of Richmond Lattimore, who instigated my endeavor to make it a still more human play in 1955 than the earlier version seemed to be in 1915. I repeat at this time the original dedication to my friend Barry Faulkner, the then young painter who helpfully watched the growth of the first version forty years ago.

CHARACTERS

Iphigenia

Pylades

Orestes

Temple Maidens

The Herdsman

Soldiers

King Thoas

Athena

IPHIGENIA IN TAURIS

SCENE: *Out of a temple by the seaside in Tauris, down steps leading to a blood-stained altar seen through its door, comes Iphigenia, the High Priestess, and stands alone on the stairway above the empty court.*

Iphigenia

Pelops, the son of Tantalus, by maiming
A chariot, won a bride, who bore him Atreus,
And Atreus had two sons, one Menelaus,
The other Agamemnon, who in turn
By Clytemnestra had a child, and I
Am she, Iphigenia.
People believe
That I was sacrificed by my own father
To Artemis, in the great pursuit of Helen,
Upon an altar near the bay of Aulis,
There where the long deep waves are caught and broken
Hither and thither by the winds, the bay
Where Agamemnon's fleet, his thousand ships
From Hellas, waited to avenge on Troy
The wrong done Menelaus through the loss
Of Helen. But a storm came up and still
Another storm and neither sea nor wind
Would favor Agamemnon. So he asked
Calchas, the soothsayer, to consult the flame.
And this is what was answered: "Agamemnon,
Captain of Hellas, there can be no way
Of setting your ships free, till the offering
You promised Artemis is given Her.
You had vowed to render Her in sacrifice
The loveliest thing each year should bear. You have owed
Long since the loveliness which Clytemnestra
Had borne to you, your daughter, Iphigenia.
Summon your daughter now and keep your word."

They sent Odysseus and his artful tongue
To lure me from my mother by pretending
That I should wed Achilles. When I had come
To Aulis, they laid hands on me. The flame
Was lit. The blow would have been struck—I saw
The knife. But Artemis deceived their eyes
With a deer to bleed for me and stole me through
The azure sky. And then She set me down
Here in this town of Tauris, this abode
Of savage men ruled by their uncouth king,
Thoas, a horseman headlong as the wind,
Who stationed me High Priestess in Her temple,
And still I serve Her on Her festal days.
Service may seem a holy word. But far
From holy are these orders I am bound
To obey, never to question: Her command that I
Must serve to Her the lives of foreigners.
It was a custom long before I came,
An ancient cruel custom. Can She hear me?
My hands prepare the victims. Other hands,
There in the inner temple, spill the blood,
Which then is poured upon this altar-stone.

(*She descends the steps into the court.*)

I dreamed last night a deathly dream. Perhaps
The morning will dispel it if I speak it—
I dreamed that I was far beyond the seas.
I seemed to be at home again in Argos,
Asleep among my maidens—when a roll
Of thunder shook the ground. I ran outside.
I watched the house. I saw the coping fall,
The cross-beams stir and yield, break and give way,
Then the whole palace plunge from roof to base,
Only one column left upright in all
My father's house. But that one stood alive,
A man with bright brown hair and breathing lips.

And then against my will my hand went out,
As it does toward strangers here condemned to die,
And touched his forehead with this fatal water—
And with water of my tears, because I knew
The dream was of Orestes and his end.
The pillar of a family is the son.
This water is the certain sign of death.
It could not mean my family next of kin;
Strophius, my uncle, never had a son.
It was my brother whom I touched with tears—
For whom I now must pour a funeral-urn,
All I can do for one so far away.

(Climbing the steps.)

Where are the women from Greece the King appointed
To live with me and help me here in the temple?
I wonder where they are. I need their help.

(She enters the temple.)

The voice of Orestes

Keep a sharp lookout. Somebody may be coming.

Pylades

(Entering by the path from the bay.)

I have looked in both directions and there's no one.

Orestes

(Following him and gazing at the temple.)

Is this the shrine of Artemis we have sailed
So many seas to find since we left Argos?
Is it, O Pylades? Is this the shrine?

Pylades

I think it is, Orestes. So do you.

Orestes

And might that stone be stained with blood of Greeks?

Pylades

If ever I saw blood—look, on the edge!

Orestes

Look, near the roof! Belongings of the dead!

Pylades

Trophies of foreigners these men have murdered!

Orestes

Careful!
O Phoebus, why must Thy oracle
Bring this on me again, the sight of blood
Again? Have I not seen enough of blood?
My mother shed my father's blood, I hers.
And then the Furies, with their eyes bloody,
Hunted me, hounded me across the land
Until at last I ran to Thee and begged
An end of all the cycles of despair
That sped me, hurled me, maddened me through Hellas.
The answer was, "Go to the Taurian country
Where Artemis, my sister, has a shrine.
Find there Her statue which had fallen down
From Heaven. Then prove yourself a man able
Enough or fortunate enough to steal it,
Stalwart enough to face all risk and bring it
Home to the holy land of Attica."
Although no more was said, I understood
That this would mean the end of my afflictions.
And here I am, O Phoebus, far from home
On a misbegotten shore—doing Thy will.
But Pylades, my fellow venturer,
Where can we turn? What man could possibly
Scale these high walls? Or climb the open stairs
And not be seen? Or force the brazen locks
Without whoever is behind them hearing?
If we are caught, it will be certain death,
Your death as well as mine. Even this waiting,
Wondering what to do, may cost our lives.
Enough of it! Enough! Back to the ship!

Pylades

What do we know of flight? How should we dare
To take a course of which our hearts know nothing?
Why should we disobey Apollo's order,
Do him dishonor? No, we shall find a way.
Come, let us leave the temple, let us look
For a dark cave to hide in. Not the ship!
By now they must have spied the ship from shore.
They'd be ahead of us, catch us and end us.
Notice the opening between those beams?
It's wide enough. Under the night's dim eye
We could drop through and hoist a wooden statue.
A coward turns away but a brave man's choice
Is danger. And by all the Gods, shall we,
Coming this far, now at the end turn back?

Orestes

I should have been the one to say those words.
Yes, let us go and find a hiding-place,
Keep faith with Phoebus and deserve his help.
Have we not youth? Youth, with its fill of strength,
Turning away from any task should be ashamed.

(*They leave by the path to the shore. A great bell rings. From the town side the Temple Maidens assemble in the courtyard.*)

A Maiden

Let those who dwell close to these Clashing Rocks
That guard the Euxine Sea,
Keep silence now before Latona's daughter,
Artemis, Goddess of the pointed hills!

(*Turning toward the temple as the bell ceases.*)

O Artemis, I come
On consecrated feet into Thy court,
I hail Thee beautiful
As the golden gleaming of Thy colonnades!

A Second Maiden

Thy priestess calls us, she who keeps Thy keys,
Who left behind, for Thee,
Her land of Hellas, the embattled towers,
The shore of horses, and the quiet fields
Wherein our fathers lived.
And we obey her call to worship Thee
In this embittered land,
Far from Eurotas and from happiness.

(*Iphigenia enters from the temple, carrying a heavy golden urn.*)

A Third Maiden

(*Crossing to Iphigenia and taking it to hold for her.*)

O daughter of the king who gathered ships
A thousand strong and led
Unnumbered men against high-towering Troy,
We heard your call and we have come to you.
Why have you summoned us?
What makes your cheek so thoughtful and so pale?
What has your tongue to tell,
That your brow is dark and bowed upon your hands?

Iphigenia

My maidens, listen. Listen while I tell
What I have seen. The Muse has veiled Her face,
And I am mourning for a dead kinsman.
Last night in a dream I saw my family's ending,
So grieve for me. I saw my brother dead.
The dream was clear. My father's house is fallen,
My race broken and gone, Orestes dead!
So grieve for all of us, for all his people.
Fate, in still scourging me, takes from all Argos
My only brother!
To the vanished dead
I shall now pour an offering, a gift
Upon the earth, commingled of the milk

Of mountain-kine and of the wine of Bacchus
And of the honey that the russet bees
Gathered, a soothing gift. This and my heart.

(To the Third Maiden.)

Give me the urn of gold which heavy holds
My tribute to the God of Death.
This urn,
Orestes, son of Agamemnon, you
Who are lying under the dark earth, I lift
And pour—for you. And may the sweetness reach
And ease your lips. Better I cannot give,
I cannot bring to you braids of my hair
And, crying, lay them down upon your grave.
Yet, though from childhood you have thought me dead,
I still can cry—far from my home and you.

A Fourth Maiden

O Lady, woe is in me for your woe,
My words are like a song
Of old which mourners in the far-off East
Chant for the dead, reciting only death,
A requiem of hell,
A wail of no returning and no hope,
Using no note of glory,
Only the desolation of the grave.

The First Maiden

Mourn for the sons of Atreus, in whose house
The hearth can never burn.
Mourn for their bitter heritage, a home
Which waits the coming of a happy king
But cannot give him welcome.
Trouble was born forever in their sky
When Pelops tricked a car
Of toppling horses out of the race for a bride.

The Third Maiden

Because of a golden lamb which long ago
Beckoned contesting men,
Mischief began to undermine your house.

The Fourth Maiden

Vengeance has made its unappeasèd way
With every dart of death
And visited your family one by one.
And now with eager hand
Fate is pursuing you. Your turn has come.

Iphigenia

Oh bitter my beginning in the womb
Of her who bore me, from the very night
When she conceived! Appointed by the Fates
To suffer in this world, I was a child
Accursed. Yet how she cherished me, her first-born,
And thrilled that I, of all the girls of Argos,
Should be a bride upon the way to Troy!
What had she borne me for and loved me for?—
To be destroyed by my own father's hand,
To come, behind the horses of delight,
Not to Achilles—but to grief and horror!
And now beside this melancholy sea
I live my days—lonely, no love, no friends,
Wife of no man and mother of no child.
I know no home. I sing no Argive song
With Argive women to the Queen of Heaven.
I weave upon the whirring loom no tale
Of Pallas routing Titans. . . . Oh, instead,
I face an altar soaked with bloody death.
I hear the cry for pity and the moans
Of men—a thing too hideous to be told.
Yet even that seems little to me now—
Now that a throne is empty and his eyes

Are done with weeping, as I wish mine were.
I who have loved him through these lonely years
Shall never see him now but as I left him,
A little baby at his mother's breast—
I who had thought to see him as a king.

The Second Maiden

(*Pointing.*)

That herdsman running, stumbling, from the beach!
What can have happened there?

(*They watch the sea-path.*)

A Herdsman

(*Entering out of breath.*)

O daughter of the house of Agamemnon,
I bring you news!

Iphigenia

Urgent enough for this
Rough outcry in the temple-yard?

The Herdsman

A ship
From sea has passed through the Symplegades!
And through the fog two fellows waded ashore,
And never was a finer offering
Than these two boys will be for Artemis!
I have been sent to tell you to make ready.

Iphigenia

Where are they from?—what country? Could you say?

The Herdsman

From Hellas, but I couldn't say which part.

Iphigenia

What were their names? Perhaps you heard their names?

The Herdsman

One of them called the other Pylades.

Iphigenia

And the one who spoke?

The Herdsman

I didn't hear his name.

Iphigenia

Where were they captured?

The Herdsman

Right there on the shore.

Iphigenia

What were you herdsmen doing on the shore?

The Herdsman

Washing our cattle there.

Iphigenia

Tell me again.
How were they captured? This is the first time
In all the years I have been living here
That any of you ever brought a Greek
To be the offering. Never a Greek.

The Herdsman

Just as we drove our cattle from the woods
To that long hollow where the curving tide
Has cut away the cliff, where the beach-men rest
From purple-fishing, one of us ahead
Came stealing back on tiptoe and he warned us,
"Those are not men but Gods! Behind that rock!
Not men but Gods!" And then another herdsman
Caught sight of them, raised up his hands and prayed,
"Palaemon, born of a Sea-Goddess, Master of Ships,
Protect us, whether these boys be the Twins
Of Battle, sons and favorites of Zeus,
Or else be brothers of the Ocean Nymphs,
Be sons of Nereus, God of Waves like Thee!"

But another jeered at us and laughed out loud,
So that I thought the Gods would turn on him.
But he was sure there must have been a wreck,
And these were sailors looking for our cave
To hide in, having heard that strangers here
Are sacrificed. And he persuaded most
Of us, and we were thinking what to do,
When one of them ran out around the rock.
Just staring, not at us or anything
That we could see, but at the air and shook
And groaned, ducking his head from side to side
Behind his arms as if he'd gone insane.
And he was calling out, sharp as a hunter,
"Look, Pylades! O look at her! O look!
There! There! Surely you see her now!—that Fiend
From Hell! And on her head look at the snakes,
Their mouths wide open, writhing for my blood!
Here comes another one! And look at that one
Up on the cliff, vomiting fire on me,
Lifting my mother's body like a rock
So she can smash it down on me and kill me!
Pylades, help me! They are all around me!"
And we could tell, by the way he jerked his head
Whenever a dog barked or a cow mooed,
That if a Fury wasn't chasing him
He thought there was in every sound he heard.
He might have knocked us flat there in a row,
We were so stunned. Instead, drawing his sword,
He lunged into our cattle like a lion,
As if they were the Furies, ripped their sides
With all his might till blood was running down,
Staining the edge. We were just untrained herdsmen
Facing expert young swordsmen; but we saw
The cattle wounded and dying and we hunted
For sticks and stones and blew our shells for help
And pretty soon farmers enough had joined us

To fight. Then, as we slowly started forward,
His madness left him. I can see him now—
Standing a moment. While I watch he drops
In a heap and foaming at the lips. Once more
We started toward him with our sticks and stones,
But still, his comrade, unafraid of us,
Leaned down to wipe the frothy mouth and laid
A piece of linen over the face to shield it—
Till suddenly the fallen man stood up,
Calm and himself again, and faced the rush
Of rocks we heaved at him like breaking waves.
We crowded in on him from every side.
He gave one groan as we surrounded him,
Ready to capture him or finish him.
And then we heard his voice ring out and say,
If this is death, let's meet it, Pylades,
Like men! Come on! Together! With our swords!"
  The metal flashed at us. We backed and tricked them
Into the hollow. There, while some of us
Would run for cover, others could throw rocks
To draw the swordsmen off and then give way
And let the first lot rally with new armfuls.
And yet we couldn't seem to hit those fellows.
I don't see how it was, with all the stones
We threw at them, that hardly one went straight.
All we could manage was to wear them down
By working round each man, aiming our volleys
Just at his sword, which, once he lost his grip,
He was too winded to pick up again.
  And when we took our prisoners to the king,
He told us we should bring them here, and you
Should get them ready for the sacrifice.
  Ask Artemis to send us more of them,
More sailor-boys from Greece, send them to Tauris,
And let more men from Hellas pay with blood
After their shouting for your blood at Aulis.

The First Maiden

This is no ordinary man who has come
From shores of Hellas to an alien shore
And battles like a God.

Iphigenia

Go back and bring me the two foreigners.
I shall be waiting for them when you come.

(*The Herdsman leaves.*)

Poor heart of mine, which always hitherto
Has been compassionate, tender toward strangers,
And even yesterday felt a quick pang
At thought of Greeks who might be lost in Tauris,
A crushing dream has changed you overnight.
For since Orestes is no more alive,
Now, where my heart was, there is only stone.
Strangers who come today, no matter who,
Will find in me a woman beyond tears.
Unhappiness, O friends, can harden us
Toward other sorrow harsher than our own.
If but some heaven-sent wind, forcing a ship
Between the Clashing Rocks, might bring me Helen,
The Helen whom I hate, and Menelaus,
That I might make of them the sacrifice,
Let a new Aulis expiate the old,
And vent my vengeance! It was Helen's fault
And his, that Greek hands lifted me at Aulis
And led me like a beast where, at the altar,
My father held the sacrificial knife.
I live it all again. My fingers, groping,
Go out to him like this and clutch his beard
And cling about his knees. I cry to him:
"It is you yourself, yourself, who brought me here,
You who deceived my maidens and my mother!
They sing my marriage-song at home, they fill
The house with happiness, while all the time

Here am I dying at my father's hands!
You led me in your chariot to take
Achilles for my lord, but here is death
And the taste of blood, not kisses, on my lips!"
  And I had left my home with my white veil
Drawn down. I had not taken in my arms
My brother—dead this day—nor kissed my sister.
I had saved all my kisses and embraces
For the man I was to marry. Even then
My heart was homesick and was faint with hope
That I should soon be back again in Argos.
  And now, O dead Orestes, you, as I,
Forfeit your heritage and lose your home.
  And what does Artemis ask of me here?—
She who forbids approach by any man
Whose hand is stained with bloodshed or with touch
Of childbirth or of burial, finds him
Unclean and bans him. She so delicate
In all these ways will yet demand the blood
Of human beings on Her altar-stone!
It cannot be. How could Latona bear
To Zeus so cruel a daughter? It is not true.
It is as false as tales of Tantalus
Feeding the Gods a child. O Artemis,
These people, being murderers themselves,
Are charging Thee with their own wickedness.
No! I will not believe it of a God!

(*She enters the temple.*)

The Second Maiden

O Clashing Rocks, under whose shadow the dark
    Threat waits, though through this cleft
Io fled safe, in her disguise as heifer
Pursued by the sharp stinging of the gadfly,
    Fled beyond Europe's land
And Europe's sea, fled safe but sick at heart,
    Away from home and kin,

Into the alien wilderness of Asia,
What sort of men would leave the holy streams
    Of Dirce, or the reeds
Green-growing in Eurotas, to explore
A bitter beach, to dare these ominous rocks
    Where the seas meet in fog,
Where Artemis, among Her colonnades
    Demanding sacrifice,
Receives upon her altar human blood?

The Fourth Maiden

Why have they urged the oarsmen of their ship
    To shake the clinging sea
With a great stroke and to accelerate
With rush of rivalry the racing wind?
    Was it to sweep the shores
For riches and to vie in bearing home,
    Each to upbuild his house,
The treasures and the trophies of the world?
That glittering hope is immemorial
    And beckons many men
To their undoing. Ever insatiate
They sail the sea and look to foreign towns
    To fill their ships with spoil.
But some men never find prosperity,
    For all their voyaging,
While others find it with no voyaging.

The Third Maiden

How have they passed the peril of the Rocks
    That Clash and of the coast
Of Phineus heavy with broken waves?
I wonder if they sailed across that reach
    Of sea where mariners
Boast to have looked on Ocean's Fifty Daughters
    Under the windowed waves,
Hand in hand dancing, circling round and singing.

The Fourth Maiden

I wonder if their rudder steered them through
That other reach of sea
Where the south wind eases and the southwest wind
Delights a sail and where the isles are white
With birds that cover them,
That rise and wheel and then curve back again,
Where the wings of ocean brood
And where Achilles races the dark waters.

The First Maiden

My Lady prayed that Fate might hither bring,
On the way home from Troy,
The cause of her great misery. Oh, would
That Helen, Helen had been blown ashore,
That on her fatal head
For punishment the holy drops might fall
And that my Lady's knife
Might find in her the fitting sacrifice!

The Second Maiden

But I have prayed for a deliverer,
Some mariner from Hellas
Able to end my grief and set me free.
Ever I go, though only in a dream,
Back to my father's house.
And few have greater riches than the joy
That comes to us in visions,
In dreams which nobody can take away.

The Third Maiden

Look, there they are! See the two men in chains!
The herdsman told the truth.
We must be quiet now for Artemis.

The Second Maiden

Can hands even from Hellas be so useless
Against this ritual!

The Fourth Maiden

O Artemis, if Tauris in Thy sight
Win honor by such gift
As never Greece would take, receive this blood!

(Entering from the temple.)

Iphigenia

Once more I must believe that Artemis
Desires this worship, once again I serve Her.

(To some of the Soldiers, who bring in the two youths.)

Loosen their hands. For in the temple court,
As in the temple during consecration,
Chains are unhallowed things.

(To the Temple Maidens, who obey.)

Enter the temple.
Prepare the altar for the sacrifice.

(Turning to the captives, with Soldiers still by them.)

I wonder who your mother was, your father,
Whether you have a sister who must lose
Her brothers and lament their bravery.
Fate comes and goes, invisible and mute,
And never whispers where Her blow shall fall.
None of us ever sees Her in the dark
Or understands Her cruel mysteries.
Tell me, unfortunate men, where are you from—
You who are far from home and yet must go
Farther away from home even than this?

Orestes

But who are you, feeling concern for us?
What could we mean to you that you should care
And make it harder for us with your pity?
What good can come from meeting death with tears?
Only a fool, finding that he must meet it,
Wishes to talk about it. If a man
Is sorry for himself, he doubles death:
Is first a coward, then a coward's corpse.

So let a man accept his destiny,
No pity and no tears. The sacrifice
Is customary here. We knew it was.

Iphigenia

One of your names was told me by a herdsman.
May I know which of you is Pylades?

Orestes

He, if it does you any good to know.

Iphigenia

And from what town in Hellas?

Orestes

Does it matter?

Iphigenia

Brothers?

Orestes

We are—in everything but birth.

Iphigenia

What is your name?

Orestes

Call me unfortunate.

Iphigenia

That would be pity's name for you.

Orestes

Then say
That I am nobody—safe from derision.

Iphigenia

Your name is too important to be told?

Orestes

Come, sacrifice my body, not my name!

Iphigenia

You will not name for me even your town?

Orestes

I am so soon a townsman of no town.

Iphigenia

Surely it is not much to tell me that.

Orestes

It is when one can say a town in Argos!

Iphigenia

Argos? Not Argos? You are not from Argos?

Orestes

My town, Mycenae, was a lordly place.

Iphigenia

Then what could make you leave it? Were you banished?

Orestes

In a way banished—banished by myselr.

Iphigenia

How good it is to see a man from Argos!

Orestes

But not to be one in your company!

Iphigenia

And let me ask about another town.

Orestes

But why this questioning?

Iphigenia

What is the news
Of that most talked-of town in the whole world?
What is the news of Troy?

Orestes

By all the Gods,
I wish that I had never heard its name!

Iphigenia

But is it true that Troy is overthrown?

Orestes

Its towers lie broken in the dust.

Iphigenia

And Helen?
Has Menelaus taken Helen back?

Orestes

Yes, to the sorrow of a noble man.

Iphigenia

She has brought me sorrow too. Where is she now?

Orestes

Gone back with him to Sparta.

Iphigenia

How I hate
The name of Helen! How all Hellas hates it!

Orestes

I have my own reason for hating it.

Iphigenia

The Achaeans are safely home, as I have heard?

Orestes

Some of them are. It would take long to tell.

Iphigenia

But tell me all you can while there is time!

Orestes

Then ask me all you can and I will answer.

Iphigenia

The soothsayer, Calchas? Is he back from Troy?

Orestes

Mycenae people say that he is dead.

Iphigenia

Praise Artemis! And is Odysseus dead?

Orestes
Not back nor dead, they say. Still wandering.

Iphigenia
Oh how I hope he never reaches home!

Orestes
Why wish him worse than he has borne already?

Iphigenia
What of Achilles?

Orestes
Dead. The marriage planned
At Aulis never happened.

Iphigenia
Those who know
Know well that it was never meant to happen.

Orestes
Knowing so much, are you yourself from Hellas?

Iphigenia
I lived in Hellas, many years ago.

Orestes
No wonder you are asking all these questions.

Iphigenia
What of that king they called The Happy King?

Orestes
I know no happy king. Whom do you mean?

Iphigenia
King Agamemnon.

Orestes
What can I say of him?
Nothing at all of him. No, do not ask me.

Iphigenia
I beg you by the Gods do me that favor.

Orestes
The news is death—his and another death.

Iphigenia
O Agamemnon! O King Agamemnon!

Orestes
Can you be kin to him, you care so much?

Iphigenia
Remembering his love of life, his pride!

Orestes
All of it ended by a woman's hand.

Iphigenia
O miserable woman! Poor, poor king!

Orestes
I pray, I beg you, ask me no more questions.

Iphigenia
Only about his queen. Is she alive?

Orestes (doggedly)
His queen is dead. Her own son killed her.

Iphigenia
Why?

Orestes
To punish her for murdering his father.

Iphigenia
It was exact of him. I pity him.

Orestes
As well you may, since no God pities him.

Iphigenia
Of Agamemnon's children, who is left?

Orestes
Electra—but her husband far from her.

Iphigenia

The one they sacrificed—what do they say?

Orestes

Nothing of her, except that she is dead.

Iphigenia

And he could kill his child—that "happy king!"

Orestes

It was a wicked war for a wicked woman,
And all the waste that has come from it is wicked.

Iphigenia

The son of the king? He too is dead in Argos!

Orestes

Not dead but not in Argos, not in Argos.

(*The Temple Maidens return to the court.*)

Iphigenia (telling them)

I dreamt Orestes dead! It was a lie!

Orestes

Dreams, lies, lies, dreams—nothing but emptiness!
Even the Gods, with all Their name for wisdom,
Have only dreams and lies and lose Their course,
Blinded, confused, and ignorant as we.
The wisest men follow their own direction
And listen to no prophet guiding them.
None but the fools believe in oracles,
Forsaking their own judgment. Those who know,
Know that such men can only come to grief.

The Second Maiden

Oh who will bring us news whether our kin
Are living or are dead?

Iphigenia

(*To Orestes.*)

For years I have had a plan which now might serve
As much to your advantage as to mine.

Joint undertakings stand a better chance
When they benefit both sides. So tell me this.
Would you, if I could win you leave to do so,
Go back to Argos, with a letter from me
Long ready for a friend of mine who lives there?
My words were written down by one who died
A victim here and yet was sorry for me,
Blaming his death on Artemis, not me.
No one had come from Hellas till you came,
No Greek who might be spared and take my letter.
But you are gentle, you are the very man
To carry it. You know the names of places
And of persons dear to me. And so I ask
Your help and in return could grant your life,
With one condition—that your friend shall pay
The price the state exacts for Artemis.

Orestes

Strange lady, you have made a fair proposal
Save in that one respect. What would my life
Be worth to me, gained by forsaking a friend?
I am the captain of this misadventure
And he the loyal shipmate who stayed by me.
A sorry ending if he paid the cost
And I rejected my own enterprise!
Your errand shall be done—but not by me.
Give him your confidence, give him your letter.
To you it makes no difference which of us
Carries your message home. To me it would make
No difference when or how my life should finish
If through continuing it, saving it,
I brought disaster on a friend and knew
No honor left in me, no faith, no love.
Besides, this man is dear to me, his life
Is even closer to me than my own.

Iphigenia

Your heart is made of gold. You must have come
From some great seed, to be so true a friend.
If only the last member of my line
Be such as you! I have a brother living,
Though face to face with him, I should not know him.
As you have chosen then, so let it be.
Your friend shall take the letter, and you prove
Your loyalty by giving him your life.

Orestes

Whose hand is it that brings the touch of death?

Iphigenia

My hand—condemned to it by Artemis.

Orestes

Your hand is still too young a hand for that.

Iphigenia

It is the law.

Orestes

That a woman shall stab men?

Iphigenia

Not that! Oh not the knife! Only the water,
The marking on the forehead—only the water!

Orestes

Whose hand then does the deed, uses the knife?

Iphigenia

Inside the temple—there are men for it.

Orestes

When I am burnt, what happens to my body?

Iphigenia

They seal the ashes in a rocky gorge.

Orestes

I wish my sister's hand might tend my body.

Iphigenia

Since she is far away and cannot hear you
Or be with you to give these services,
I shall attend to them. I am from Argos.
I will do everything that she might do,
Will bring rich robes to be your final clothing
And funeral ornaments to set about you
And yellow oil to pour, cooling and clean,
Upon the embers. I will melt your ashes
In gold that bees collect from mountain-flowers.
You shall be pure and sweet.
While I am gone
To find my letter, do not think ill of me.

(*To the Soldiers.*)

Keep guard, soldiers, without binding these men.

(*To herself, pausing as she leaves the court.*)

Oh, if at last my letter should arrive
In Argos and be opened by his own
Beloved hand, a letter never dreamed of,
Then he would listen through my opening grave
And hear my living lips cry out to him.

(*She leaves, passing around the temple.*)

The First Maiden

O you whose head must feel this water's touch,
My heart goes out to you!

Orestes

Have hope for him, instead of pitying me.

The First Maiden

My heart both pities you and hopes for him
That he may safely reach
His father's country and be happy there.

Pylades

Could I desert a friend and still be happy?

The First Maiden

Or I help pitying a man who dies?

The Fourth Maiden

The one who lives will be the one I pity.

The Third Maiden

Which is the sadder fate?

The Fourth Maiden

I cannot tell. I watch and cannot tell
Whether to pity you, or you, the more.

(*The Temple Maidens leave the courtyard.*)

Orestes

What is it, Pylades? What puzzles you?

Pylades

What do you think it is that puzzles me?

Orestes

That woman and the way she put her questions.
The sort of questions: the defeat of Troy,
The Achaeans' homecoming, what happened to Calchas,
To Achilles, and her being so concerned
At Agamemnon's death and then inquiring
About his wife and children. I believe
It true that she herself belongs in Argos
Or she would never send a letter there
And care about occurrences in Argos
As if they flowed within her very veins.

Pylades

Yes, that is what at first had puzzled me,
And then I thought it natural enough
That in a place even half civilized
People should care about the fate of kings.
But that was not what puzzled me, not that.

Orestes

If we put our heads together, we could surely—

Pylades

How can you wrong me, thinking I would live
And leave you here to die? I came with you.
I shall continue with you to the end,
Or I could never show my face again
On an Argive hill or in a Phocian valley
But to be pointed out and rightly spurned
As one who had betrayed a friend. People
Might say worse things than that, the worst
An evil mind could think of to enjoy:
That I had wished or even caused your death
To benefit, as husband of your sister,
By my inheritance—to win your throne.
Such thoughts are frightening, but worse my shame
In your imagining that I might leave you.
If you meet knife and flame, then so do I.
I am your friend and there's no more to say.

Orestes

How can you be my friend and yet refuse me?
The load I bear can never be laid down—
And would you add to it by lightening yours?
All the contempt you imagine from men's hearts
And tongues, falling on you, would fall on me
In my own heart from my own conduct, if I let
The service you have done me bring you harm.
What has Fate left me of my life to cherish
But a good ending? As for you, my comrade,
You have not any right to choose to die.
You have the blessing of your fortunate blood
To make you wish to live. I can but pray
That, by your living, solace may be brought
To my ill-fated family. Pylades,
Once home again and with your wife, my sister,

Give me my happiness by having a son
In whom my name shall live, and through your children
Build up once more the house of Agamemnon.
Go back, I say, and make my home your home.
You will be there in Hellas, on the shore
Where Argive horsemen ride. Give me your hand
And swear to me that you will build my tomb,
Will set memorials in it and will ask
My sister for a lock of her long hair
To lay with them. Tell her that I was led
Before this altar by a gentle hand,
A woman's hand, a woman born in Argos,
And how at last my blood was purified.
   O Pylades, be gentle to my sister!
And so goodbye, my best and closest friend.
When we were boys, we loved sharing our sports.
You rode the hills with me And now in manhood
You are the one who has shared the heartache with me
When treacherous Phoebus through his oracle
First lied to me, then tricked me, luring me far
From home, lest watchful eyes in Hellas see
That Gods as well as men break promises.
I trusted Him, with all my faith and will,
Even, at His command, killing my mother,
And in return He has forsaken me.

Pylades

I shall obey your will, though not my own;
Shall build your tomb in Hellas. Your heart knows
That I shall love your sister all my life.
And, close to you in your life, my heart knows
That it shall hold you closer in your death—
If death it be. Gods, in mysterious ways,
Never explaining, mask the face of life,
Behind what looks like death, disguising life,
And then revealing it.

Orestes

The time is gone
When Gods might show that face. For she has come.

Iphigenia

(Returning to the temple by the town-path and addressing the Attendants who follow her.)

Precede me into the temple and be ready.

(The Attendants enter the temple.)

Here is my letter, safe within these folds.
But I have wondered. A man who has been in danger
When he comes out of it forgets his fears,
And sometimes he forgets his promises.
Might it not happen that your friend, intent
Upon his own concerns again, forget
How very much this letter means to me?

Orestes

And what would you suggest, to ease your mind?

Iphigenia

His solemn vow to take this where I say.

Orestes

And will you make a vow balancing his?

Iphigenia

To do what, or undo what?

Orestes

To make sure
He be allowed to leave this deathly place.

Iphigenia

How could he keep his vow, unless he leave?

Orestes

What makes you think the king will let him sail?

Iphigenia

I can persuade the king and will myself
Go to the ship and see your friend aboard.

Orestes

Then word the vow as you would have him make it.

Iphigenia

You promise the delivery of my letter?

Pylades

I promise the delivery of your letter.

Iphigenia

I promise you the king will let you leave.

Pylades

In whose name do you swear?

Iphigenia

By Artemis,
Here in Her Temple—and implore Her help.

Pylades

And I by Zeus Himself, by Heaven's King.

Iphigenia

And what if you should fail to keep your word?

Pylades

Then may I never again set eyes on Argos.
And what if you should fail in keeping yours?

Iphigenia

Then may I never again set foot in Argos.

Pylades

But we forget one possibility.

Iphigenia

Which might affect the keeping of your vow?

Pylades

How could I keep my vow if this should happen—
If we were wrecked by a storm, torn by a reef,
If we were sunk and everything went down,
And if my life were saved but not the letter.
If that should happen, how could I keep my word?

Iphigenia

In any plan, two ways improve on one.
So I will tell you, slowly, line by line,
The contents of my letter, which, if need be,
You are to tell my friend. Then he will know.
For either you will place it in his hand
And the written words will speak to him or else,
If they are lost, your voice will be their echo.

Pylades

That is a surer way, for both of us.
So whom am I to find for you in Argos?
What shall I say to him?

Iphigenia

Say this to him.
Say to Orestes, son of Agamemnon,
"A greeting comes from one you think is dead."
Tell him, "Your sister is not dead at Aulis
But is alive."

Orestes

Alive? Iphigenia?
Oh, no! Unless the dead come back again!

Iphigenia

You are looking at her now, for I am she.
But let me finish what I ask of him.
"O brother, come and save me from a life
As priestess in a loathsome ritual—
Save me from dying in this lonely land."

Orestes

Where am I, Pylades? What am I hearing?

Iphigenia

"Lest memory of me should always haunt you."
The name, you must repeat it, is Orestes.

Orestes

I hear a God!

Iphigenia

You hear only a woman.

Orestes

I hear a woman—and I hear a God!
Let me hear more! I hear a miracle!

Iphigenia

Then tell him, "Artemis put out Her hand
And spared my life at Aulis, leaving a deer
To bleed instead." And tell him this, "My father,
Not looking when he struck, believed me dead.
Artemis brought me here." The letter ends.

Pylades

No word was ever easier to keep!
Lady, keep yours or not, I keep mine now!
I give you this, Orestes, from your sister!

(*Enter the Temple Maidens.*)

Orestes

How can I look at letters! Let me look—
Oh let me stare at you whom I had lost!
Oh let me touch you with my hands and prove
That you are real and hold you close, close!

The Third Maiden

Do not lay hands, whoever you may be,
Upon a vestment sacred
To Artemis! Do not profane that robe!

Orestes

You are my sister, you are my father's daughter,
And nature will not let you turn away
From your own brother given back to you.

Iphigenia

Ah, you would have me think that you are he.
Orestes is not here. He is in Argos.

Orestes

Poor sister, not in Argos! I am here!

Iphigenia

You mean Tyndareus was your mother's father?

Orestes

Yes, and my father's grandfather was Pelops.

Iphigenia

What are you saying? How can I believe you?

Orestes

By asking me more questions—about home.

Iphigenia

Say anything—say anything at all.

Orestes

Electra used to tell us about Atreus,
About Thyestes, how they came to quarrel.

Iphigenia

The fight they had over the golden lamb!

Orestes

The tapestry you made of it, yourself.

Iphigenia

Are you Orestes? Is it really you?

Orestes

Another tapestry you made, of Helios
Changing His course. Have you forgotten that?

Iphigenia

I can remember every single thread.

Orestes

And the bath perfumes, a present for your wedding,
Sent by your mother to Aulis—you remember?

Iphigenia

I live each bitter moment of that day.

Orestes

The lock of hair you sent back to your mother?

Iphigenia

I meant it for my own memorial
To mark a grave where I could never lie.

Orestes

The keepsake in your room! Do you remember
The ancient spear, the one Pelops had used
On Oenomaus, when he won from him
Hippodamia as a bride from Pisa?

Iphigenia

It is, it is! Orestes! O my brother!
My home has come to me from far away,
For you have come, I have you in my arms.

Orestes

And I have you in mine, whom I thought dead.
No wonder that our eyes are blind with tears,
Of joy, not sorrow—yet of sorrow too.

Iphigenia

You were a baby when I sailed away,
Lifted to watch me, held up by your nurse
To wave goodbye. And now those little arms
I saw reach out have come to me, grown strong
To comfort me! How can I tell my joy?
There is no language sweet enough to tell it.
There is no joy like this. There never was.

Orestes

And there must never be an end of it.

Iphigenia

I am bewildered. And I cannot think
What I should say, my friends. I cannot think
Of anything but joy—except a fear
That he might vanish as he came. O Argos!
My heart is full of my beloved Argos,
Of everybody who belongs to Argos,
And of my brother born and bred in Argos
To be a living light honoring Argos!

Orestes

How could the happiness we both were born for
Become unhappiness?

Iphigenia

Unhappiness
Began for me when my unhappy father
Lifted a knife and drew it toward my throat.

Orestes

I was not there, and yet how plain I see you!

Iphigenia

And do you see what I remember there?
The treachery, the misery, the shame!
After the trickery, the vanishing
Of all my dreams! Not to Achilles' arms
I went, circled with songs, but, shaken with sobs,
I felt the hot flame from the altar-stone
And the cold water trickled on my head.

Orestes

O desolate daughter of a desolate father!
I see his face. I see his haunted face!

Iphigenia

But why feel pity for the pitiless man
Who caused all this?

Orestes

And might have caused today
Your leading your own brother to the grave.

Iphigenia

Some God prevented. But I came so near,
My hand so nearly set the final seal,
That I still shake as though you lay here dead.
We have seen the beginning of a miracle.
We found each other and my hand was spared
From signalling your death. How can we now
Fulfill the miracle, make it complete?
How can I save you from some other hand
And speed you safely homeward from this place?
There will be many hands, and many swords,
For you to face. How could you match them all?
A giant's task, too much for any man!
There are no weapons possible but wits,
And yet I see you stand there dazed as I.
Could you outrun them when they follow you,
Escape them on an inland wooded trail?
Or would a dash through breakers be the way?
Would you be safer trusting to the trail
Or to the ship? Oh, I can see you losing
Your way on land, risking a thousand deaths.
The countryside is full of savage men.
The ship is better, even that sharp cleft
Between the Clashing Rocks. Yes, risk the sea.
You challenged it, came through it. Having once
Met it and mastered it, you can again.
And so let fly your oars. Yes, risk the sea,
Take to the ship—though who can surely tell
If God or man shall steer you through the waves
To a safe landing, or if Fate shall grant
Argos the benison of your return?
Or me—who knows?—the sweet surprise of mine!

The Third Maiden
I have heard marvelous tales from story-tellers,
But nothing to compare
With this event which my own eyes have seen.

Pylades
Orestes, it was natural and right
For you and for your sister to compare
Old memories, but surely it's high time
We think of nothing else but our escape
From this grim place and how to manage it.
No man, when Fortune beckons him, should wait
A single instant. He should follow her.

Orestes
Meet her halfway, you mean, more than halfway,
Since every God helps him who helps himself.

Iphigenia
But first—I cannot wait—I have to hear!
Oh tell me just a word about my sister—
About Electra! Tell me about Electra!

Orestes
This is the husband who has made her happy.

Iphigenia
This man? But who. . . .

Orestes
A Phocian. Strophius' son.

Iphigenia
Then he is Atreus' grandson! He's our kinsman!

Orestes
Your cousin—my one friend.

Iphigenia
Not even born
When I left home to die.

Orestes

He is the son
Of Strophius in old age.

Iphigenia

I welcome you,
My sister's husband.

Orestes

And my more than brother.

Iphigenia

But oh our mother? You have not said why—

Orestes

I said enough—I said she killed our father.

Iphigenia

You have not told me why.

Orestes

Then do not ask me.

Iphigenia

May I not ask if you are king of Argos?

Orestes

Not king but exile. Menelaus is king.

Iphigenia

When you most needed him, he drove you out?

Orestes

Not he. The Furies—the avenging Fiends.

Iphigenia

Your madness on the beach—it was the Fiends?

Orestes

Anyone seeing me might think it madness.

Iphigenia

Still chasing you because you killed our mother?

Orestes

They try to choke me with my mother's blood!

Iphigenia

What brought you here?

Orestes

Phoebus—His oracle.

Iphigenia

Why should He choose this place?

Orestes

Oh let me tell
My bitter narrative from end to end.
After my hand had unforgivably
Punished my mother's unforgivable sin,
Down on my head they came, the Avenging Furies,
The nameless Fiends. Then Phoebus ordered me
To Athens that I might explain to Them
In the Tribunal Zeus had sanctified
To Ares when she answered ancient charges.
When I arrived there, none of all my friends
Received me. They avoided me at first
As one unclean. Later they pitied me
And gave me food in the same room with them
But at a separate table where they let
My meals be served when theirs were, sent me a cup
When their love-bowl was passed, but then would turn
Away and would not look at me nor speak
To me—because I was a murderer. . . .
I tried to act as though I did not care,
But sad and lonely when I thought of her
Whom I had killed, I drank a bitter cup.
I am told Athenians commemorate
My trial with a Service of the Pitcher,
Everyone drinking his own cup in silence. . . .
While I was facing judgment on that hill,

I on one flagging and across from me
The eldest of the Avengers charging me
With murder, Phoebus rose to my defense.
It was His eloquence that saved my life,
Persuading Pallas, in the chair, with votes
Cast evenly for and against me, that she add
Her own vote for me—which acquitted me.
  Some of the Fiends, persuaded, went to found
A cellar temple under the Tribunal.
Others denounced the verdict as unfair
And flew at me in such a vicious frenzy
That I ran back for help again from Phoebus,
Faint with despair fell down upon my knees
And swore to starve myself to death unless
The God who had ruined me would rescue me.
  Out pealed His voice over the golden tripod,
Bidding me find among the Taurians
Their Artemis of wood carven in Heaven
But fallen on their coast and, stealing it,
Establish it for Grecian worshippers
In Attica.
            Help me to do this thing
And to fulfil His mission. Help me, sister!
Once I have carried home in these two hands
The image of the Goddess, I am rid
Of madness! And I urge you with a gift
Of rugged rowers rowing you home to Argos!
O my own sister, for our family's sake,
Help me to save that family and ourselves!
Unless you help me take the image back,
This very day our family's name shall die.

The Fourth Maiden

Some God is visiting ancestral sin
    On the house of Tantalus.

Iphigenia

How I had dreamed, long, long before your coming,
Of you and of my country! How my prayer
Joins yours for the renewal of our breed—
Even of his whose hand reached for my blood!
Now that no blood of yours stains my own hand,
I have no anger left, but only hope
That in your life the family name shall live.
  But if you leave me, taking Artemis,
When the king sees the empty pedestal,
What can I say? How can my life be saved
Unless, with one quick stroke seizing the image,
We flee together to your leaping deck?
If we succeed, what happiness for me!
But even if I fail, you need not fail.
My life is little. I would gladly die
To earn your safety and your reaching home.
If a man die, a house, a name, is lost.
But if a woman die, what does it matter?

Orestes

It mattered when my mother died! If now
You also were to die because of me—!
Whatever happen, we shall share one fate,
Alive in Greece, or here together dead.
  But by all signs, the Gods are on our side.
If Artemis were not, why should it be
Her Brother's oracle commanding me
To bring Her image back? She wishes it!
Here in Her Temple, in Her very presence,
Has come the omen of my finding you!
Yes, we are being guided by the Gods!

Iphigenia

The king will kill us if we steal the statue.

Orestes

Then why not kill the king?

Iphigenia

Anger the Gods
Again? He has been kind to me.

Orestes

Why not,
To save our lives, take chances with the Gods?

Iphigenia

I like your boldness. But it cannot be.

Orestes

What if you hid me somewhere in the temple?

Iphigenia

To steal out after dark?

Orestes

Since I must steal,
The day for honest men, the night for thieves.

Iphigenia

Guards are on watch inside.

Orestes

How else are we—

Iphigenia

We might—

Orestes

Might what?

Iphigenia

Make use of your misfortune.

Orestes

Women have ways of changing ill to good.

Iphigenia

I shall denounce you as a matricide.

Orestes

Make use of any good you find in that.

Iphigenia
As one unworthy to be sacrificed.

Orestes
I understand—but not how it would serve us.

Iphigenia
You are unclean—cannot be purified—

Orestes
What will that do for us?

Iphigenia
except by deep
Sea-water, beyond stain, off from the shore.

Orestes
Yes, but our mission, you forget the statue—
The reason for our coming here.

Iphigenia
She too,
Having been soiled by your approach, must be
Washed clean, the image too!

Orestes
I see it now.
The inlet where the ship—

Iphigenia
strains at the leash.

Orestes
And you will bring the image there yourself!

Iphigenia
Nobody ever touches it but me.

Orestes
But Pylades? Is he a murderer too?

Iphigenia
He aided you. He also must be cleansed.

Orestes

A story for the guards—but for the king?

Iphigenia

In any case I could not keep it from him.
So he shall hear it and shall be persuaded.

Orestes

Fifty stout oars are waiting for the word.

Iphigenia

That is the part of it I leave to you.

Orestes

I have but one suggestion. Do these women
Realize how much their loyalty might mean?
Women know women. Make your plea to them.
And after that we are in the hands of Heaven.

Iphigenia

O friends who have been near and dear to me,
It may depend upon your carefulness
Whether or not I reach my home and kin.
A woman knows how much her weakness needs
The sympathy and help of other women,
Their understanding and their loyalty.
I ask you only this, that you say nothing
Of what has happened here, that you keep silent.
The stillest tongue can be the truest friend.
We three must take a hair's-breadth chance between
Capture and death, deliverance and home.
But if we do escape, then we shall work
For your deliverance, for you and you
To share our happiness at home in Hellas
And you and you. Holding your hand, I ask you—
Kissing your cheek. Clasping your knees, I ask you—
And you I ask by love of your two parents.

(*To the Second Maiden.*)

And you by love of the child you left behind.
Who will say yes to me? Who could say no
When it might cost my brother's life and mine?

The First Maiden

Rely on me, dear Lady.

The Second Maiden

And on me.

The Third Maiden

We shall do everything we can to help.

The Fourth Maiden

By Zeus we pledge silence and loyalty.

Iphigenia

May Heaven reward the hearts behind those words!

(*To Orestes and Pylades.*)

Now for your part—and yours—inside the temple.
The king will soon arrive and will be asking
Whether the strangers have been sacrificed.

(*Orestes and Pylades enter the temple.*)

O gallant Goddess, having saved me once
At Aulis from my father's deadly hand,
Save with me now my brother and his friend,
Lest Phoebus be disproved because of Thee
And men forsake His oracle. O come
In gracious might away from this bleak place,
Away from gloom, to the lovely light of Athens.

(*She follows into the temple.*)

The First Maiden

O sad-voiced ocean-bird, heard in the foam
Low by the rocky ledge
Singing a note unhappy hearts can hear,
The song of separation from your mate,
The moan of separation,

I have no wings to seek like you, but I
Can sing a song like you,
A song of separation from my mate.

The Second Maiden

At home in Hellas now my kinsmen gather
Where Artemis is due
To bless the new-born from her Cynthian hill
And soothe the mothers with the cooling palm
And bay and olive-tree,
Where once Latona loved the winding streams
And watched the rounded pools
White with the song-like motion of the swans.

The Third Maiden

Alas, the falling tears, the towers fallen,
The taking of our towns!
Alas, the clang of bright and angry spears
Which drove me, captive, to an alien ship,
Whence I was sold away
To be an exile here, a handmaiden
With Agamemnon's daughter,
Doomed to the bloody rites of Artemis!

The Fourth Maiden

And at this altar where the sacrifice
Is not of sheep but men,
I envy those unhappy from their birth,
For to be bred and seasoned in misfortune
Is to be iron to it,
But there is something in the pang of change
More than the heart can bear,
Unhappiness remembering happiness.

The Second Maiden

Lady, a ship is here to take you home,
And in the rowers' ears
Pan shall be sounding all his pointed notes,

Great mountains echoing to His little reed,
    And Phoebus on His lyre
Shall strike profound the seven strings and sing
    To you of Attica,
Shall sing to you of home and lead you there.
Oar after oar shall dip and carry you,
    Lady, away from us,
Oar after oar shall push the empty waves
Wider, wider, leaving us lonely here,
    Leaving us here without you,
And forward over the unceasing bow
    The sail shall faster run,
Ever refilling with the unspent wind.

The First Maiden

Oh to fly swifter than the wingèd sun
    Upon his dazzling track!—
And not to let my golden light be folded
Until I touch my house, my roof, my room,
    From which I used to go
To noble marriages and take my place
    In the bright company,
Give them my hands and circle round and dance
And always try to be the loveliest,
    Under my mother's gaze,
In my unrivalled radiance of attire
And in the motion of my hands and feet,
    While my embroidered veil
I would hold closely round me as I danced
    And bowed and hid my cheek
Under the shadow of my clustering curls.

(*Enter King Thoas with Soldiers.*)

Thoas

Where is my guardian of the temple gate,
My Grecian girl? Where are the foreigners?
Am I too late to see the sacrifice?
Are the victims' bodies being burnt already?

The Fourth Maiden

She is coming out herself and she will tell you.

(*Iphigenia appears in the temple-door, carrying the wooden Artemis.*)

Thoas

(*Starting up the stairs.*)

What does this mean, daughter of Agamemnon?
Why have you moved the Goddess from her place?

Iphigenia

O King, stand back—stay back beyond the threshold!

Thoas

But what has happened that would call for this?

Iphigenia

Back from contamination! I am abrupt.

Thoas

Speak bluntly to me. What?

Iphigenia

The offerings
You sent us for the Goddess are impure.

Thoas

How do you know? What makes you think—

Iphigenia

She turned
Away from them. She moved when they came near.

Thoas

Mightn't it be a little bit of earthquake
That moved Her?

Iphigenia

No. She moved of Her own will
And even for a moment shut Her eyes.

Thoas
Because their hands were blood-stained? Was it that?

Iphigenia
It was Her divination of their guilt.

Thoas
You mean they'd killed a Taurian on the beach?

Iphigenia
Their guilt was with them when they came—the crime
Of killing their own kin.

Thoas
What kin?

Iphigenia
Mother
Of one of them—a murder they had planned.

Thoas
O great Apollo, what barbarian
Would do the thing these Greeks have done!

Iphigenia
Greeks once
But now disowned by Greeks, driven from Hellas.

Thoas
Even so, why bring the Goddess out?

Iphigenia
Defiled,
She must be purified, be cleaned again
By the touch of Her own sky.

Thoas
How could you know
What sort of crime these fellows had committed?

Iphigenia
I saw Her turn from them. I asked them why.

Thoas

You are a Greek, quick-witted, a true Greek.

Iphigenia

They are Greek too, tried to propitiate me
With welcome news.

Thoas

Of Argos?

Iphigenia

Of my brother,
News of Orestes.

Thoas

Thought they could weaken you.

Iphigenia

News that my father is alive and prospers.

Thoas

But you were firm. You didn't let your feelings—

Iphigenia

What should I feel toward any Greek but hate?

Thoas

How shall we deal with them?

Iphigenia

By temple rules.

Thoas

Something besides the pitcher and the knife?

Iphigenia

Complete immersion, for a sin like theirs.

Thoas

In the bubbling spring? Or is salt water best?

Iphigenia

The sea is the absorbent of all evil.

Thoas

Artemis says the sea?

Iphigenia

I say the sea.

Thoas

Breakers are handy—just beyond the wall.

Iphigenia

But these especial rites are secret rites.

Thoas

Then choose your place; no one shall trespass on you.

Iphigenia

And I shall have to wash the Goddess too.

Thoas

Can a Goddess be defiled, the same as people?

Iphigenia

Why did I have to bring Her from the temple?

Thoas

You are a pious woman and I thank you.

Iphigenia

Then will you issue orders for me?

Thoas

Name them.

Iphigenia

First have the strangers bound with rope.

Thoas

But why?

Where could they go?

Iphigenia

O King, beware of Greeks!

Thoas

(*To his Soldiers.*)

Bind them.

Iphigenia

And have them brought to me.

Thoas

And bring them.

Iphigenia

But cover both their heads with heavy cloth.

Thoas

To keep even the Sun from seeing them?

Iphigenia

Send soldiers with me.

Thoas

Take your pick of them.

Iphigenia

And have a herald tell all Taurians—

Thoas

To what?

Iphigenia

To stay indoors till this is done.

Thoas

One step outdoors and they would be polluted.

Iphigenia

By matricide!

Thoas

(*To Attendants.*)

Go tell the herald this.

Iphigenia

Indoors they stay.

Thoas

My people do concern you!

Iphigenia

The one I am most concerned about—

Thoas

Who? Me?

Iphigenia

Has helpful work to do, inside the temple.

Thoas

To—?

Iphigenia

Purify it with pine smoke from torches.

Thoas

The temple shall be sweet for your return.

Iphigenia

When they come out—

Thoas

What shall I do?

Iphigenia

Hold up
Your sleeve and shield your face.

Thoas

From the contagion.

Iphigenia

And if I seem delayed—

Thoas

How shall I tell?

Iphigenia

Feel no surprise, be patient.

Thoas

You must do,
Carefully, everything the Goddess wants.

Iphigenia

I trust that I can serve Her wish.

Thoas

And mine.
(The temple doors open for an emerging procession.)

Iphigenia

And here they come, the strangers in their robes,
And lambs whose blood is used instead of theirs,
And burning torches and the instruments
Needed for purifying them and Her.
Taurians, turn away from the pollution.
Gate-tenders, open the gates, then wash your hands.
Men who want wives, women who want children,
Avoid contagion, keep away, away!

(Holding the image high.)

O Virgin Goddess, if the waves can wash
And purge the taint from these two murderers
And wash from Thee the tarnishing of blood,
Thy dwelling shall be clean and we be blest! . . .
To Thee and the All-Wise my silent prayer.

(She signals. The procession moves down the stairs. Carrying the image, she leads the Soldiers and victims from the foot of the stairs across the court and out toward the sea. Thoas enters the temple with Attendants, leaving in the courtyard only the Temple Maidens.)

The Second Maiden

Latona bore one day a golden Child,
Brother of Artemis,
Phoebus, the darling of the vales of Delos—

The First Maiden
Whose little fingers hovered on the harp
And pulled at archery.

The Second Maiden
Up from His birthplace, to Parnassus' top
The Mother brought Her Boy—

The First Maiden
Where Dionysus vaults the waterfall.

The Third Maiden
There, hidden coiling in the leafy laurels,
A serpent with bright scales
And blood-red eyes, a creature born of Earth,
Guarded the cave that held Earth's oracle.
Phoebus, beholding it, leaped up
Out of His Mother's arms, a little Child,
And struck the serpent dead—

The Second Maiden
And on that day began His prophecies.

The Fourth Maiden
O Phoebus, having won the golden throne
And tripod of the truth,
Out of the very center of the Earth,
Thou couldst hear wisdom; and Thy voice conveyed,
Accompanied by all
The run and ripple of Castalian springs,
The deepest prophecies
That ever Earth heard whispered out of Heaven.

The Third Maiden
But Earth had wished to save the oracle
For Themis, Her own daughter,
And so in anger bred a band of dreams
Which in the night should be oracular
To men, foretelling truth.

And this impaired the dignity of Phoebus
    And of His prophecies.

The Second Maiden

And the baby God went hurrying to Zeus,
Coaxed with His little hands and begged of Zeus
    To send the dreams away.

The First Maiden

And Zeus was very pleased to have His Son
Come straight to Him with troubles. His great brow
    Decided with a nod
That Phoebus have his prize restored to Him,
    In spite of angry Earth,
His throne, His listening throng, His golden voice . . .

The Fourth Maiden

That throats of night be stricken straightway mute
    And plague mankind no more,
That shapes of night no longer hold their power
To foretell truth in syllables of gloom
    And haunt men's aching hearts—
That men be freed from the prophetic dark
    And every shrouded form
And listen only to the lips of light.

A Soldier

(*Entering headlong on the sea-path, wounded and breathless.*)
O temple ministrants and temple guards,
Where is King Thoas? Open all your gates
And call King Thoas out! Summon the king!

The First Maiden

Am I allowed to ask why so much noise?

The Soldier

The two young prisoners have broken free,
With Agamemnon's daughter joining them,
And are taking Artemis aboard their ship!

The Second Maiden

You have gone mad to dream of such a thing!

The First Maiden

A likely story! If you want the king,
He has left the temple. Go and look for him.

The Soldier

Tell me which way, because I have to find him.

The First Maiden

I do not know which way.

The Third Maiden

None of us noticed.

The Second Maiden

Go look for him, tell him your crazy story.

The Soldier

O treacherous women, you're deceiving me,
You're in the plot yourselves!

The Third Maiden

You make no sense.
What are these men to us? Go try the palace.

The Soldier

Not till I know what's happening right here.
Not till the keepers of the inner shrine
Have answered me! Ho! You inside! Unbar
The door! Is the king there? Tell him to hurry!
Tell him a soldier's out here—with bad news!

(*He beats at the door. The door opens and Thoas appears.*)

Thoas

Why are you making this ungodly uproar?
Everyone's in a panic!

The Soldier

These women lied!
They said that you had left, they lied to me,
Tried not to let me find you!

Thoas

What do you mean?
Why should they wish—

The Soldier

That will come later. Listen,
Oh listen first to me, listen to this!
Your Priestess, Iphigenia! She has freed
The prisoners! They've stolen Artemis!
The ocean ceremony was a trick.

Thoas

But why should she be playing tricks on me?

The Soldier

To save Orestes. Yes, I said Orestes!

Thoas

Orestes? What Orestes? Not her brother?

The Soldier

Whom we had brought to you for Artemis.

Thoas

But that's impossible! How can I grasp it?

The Soldier

There isn't time to grasp it! You must say
What's to be done about it! You must order
Galleys to cut ahead of them and catch them!

Thoas

There's no escape for them. Our boats are out there,
So tell me how it happened. Everything.

The Soldier

It was just when we had reached the bend of shore
Hiding their ship that Agamemnon's daughter
Made signs for us to drop the rope which bound
The men, to leave them and fall back. She said
That she was ready to begin the rites
And light the mystic flame to bless the sea.
But when she took the cord and led the boys
Beyond the curve, we had a sudden feeling
Something was wrong. We didn't know what to do.
We heard her voice call high mysterious words
We'd never heard and thought that this must be
The prayer she had to use for cleansing sin.
And then we waited a long time. At last
We were afraid the men had broken loose
And killed her and escaped. And still we waited,
Because you had forbidden us to look,
But we suddenly decided to find out
And hurried to the inlet.
There we saw
The ship from Hellas swaying near the beach,
And fitted in the tholes were fifty oars
Like feathers in a wing. And the two youths
Were waist-deep by the stern. Sailors held poles
For keeping the bow steady, others hauled
The anchor up. The rest had hands along the ropes
Of a ladder hanging from the rail to help
The Priestess. But we seized her in the water,
Tugged at the ladder, ripped their rudder-oar
Away from them to cripple them and cried
To the fellow facing us, "What kind of man
Are you, stealing our Priestess and our Goddess?"
"I am Orestes, son of Agamemnon,
I am her brother! Now you have the truth!
And she is bound for Greece, out of which land
I lost her long ago—bound home!" We tried

To hold her, tried to drag her from their hands,
Which is the way I came by this and this.
He struck my face, first one side, then the other.
They had no weapons, we had none. We used
Our fists and they their fists, and some their feet
With kicks well-aimed at us from where they stood
Above us—at our heads and hearts. We fought
And fought till we were winded. Then, with bruises
And cuts and blood-filled eyes, we climbed the cliff
And from above we pelted them with rocks.
But the Greek archers had brought up their bows
And with their arrows kept us at a distance.
  Then when a giant wave bore in on them,
Orestes quickly lifted up his sister
Out of the rush of it. Holding her high
On his left shoulder, plunging stride by stride,
He caught a ladder, climbed aboard the ship
And set her safe on deck. And she, she held—
She had it still—the statue out of Heaven,
The image of the Daughter of High Zeus.
  We heard a glad voice ringing through the ship,
"O mariners of Hellas, grip your oars
And clip the sea to foam! O let your arms
Be strong, for we have won, have won, have won
What we set out to win! Soon we shall leave
The jagged Clashing Rocks behind! Pull hard!"
  A shout of joy resounded and the ship
Quivered with dipping oars and shot ahead.
But this was only while the shelter lasted;
For at the harbor-mouth the sharp wind threw her
High on a heavy swell shoreward again.
Her oarsmen rallied, strained, but every time
They made a gain, a great wave drove her back.
Then Agamemnon's daughter stood and prayed:
"Oh save me, Artemis, from this grim place!
Help us all home to Hellas! And forgive

Theft of the image at Thy Brother's bidding!
As He is dear to Thee, so mine to me!"
The sailors roared their echoes to her prayer,
And bent their bodies and their great bare arms
And shoulders, swinging like the sea,
To the boatswain's cry. But closer to the cliff,
Closer they drew and closer still. And some
Sprang out into the water and began
Trying to fasten hold on the sharp rocks
With ropes. And then our soldiers sent me here
To tell you what has happened. So bring cord
And chains, O King, for if the sea stays rough,
There's not a chance that they can get away.
Poseidon, Ocean's God, mindful of Troy,
The city which He loved, is punishing
The impious children of her enemies,
And will deliver to the King of Tauris
The son and daughter of the King of Argos—
That daughter who, forgetful now of Aulis,
Betrays the Goddess who was good to her.

The First Maiden

O Lady, Lady! Fate is yielding you
To Taurian hands again.
You and your brother surely now shall die.

Thoas

Come, citizens, and be uncivilized!
Leap on your horses! Whip them to the beach!
There we can wait until a billow splits
That ship from Hellas. Then go after them!
And hunt them down, every damned dog of them!
Do this for Artemis. And some of you
Go launch my galleys, lest one man of them
Should die untortured! Run them down by sea
And land! Go hurl them from the cliffs!
Oh catch them, crush them, crucify them—kill them!

And as for you, you miserable women,
Count on the punishment which you have earned
By treachery! That punishment can wait—
With this to do. But oh when this is done!

(Above the confusion appears, with instant dominion, Pallas Athena.)

Athena

Quiet, King Thoas! What is all this tumult?
Hold the chase back and listen to Athena.
Hold all your soldiers back. Yes, all of them.
Apollo sent Orestes to your country
To set him free from the Avenging Furies,
Ordered him, through an oracle, to bring
Iphigenia home again to Argos
And the sacred statue home to Her own land.
You have the story. But there's one addition—
The fact that this Orestes you would hunt
Is gliding on a comfortable sea.
Poseidon made it smooth. I asked Him to.
Orestes! Gods are heard at any distance.
Though you are far away, you still can hear me.
Do this. Take back your sister and the statue
Safely to Hellas. Pause at God-built Athens.
Then, passing through, continue to the end
Of Attica and find a holy place
Close to Carystus' hill, a place called Halae.
There build a temple. There set up the image,
That men may flock to Her with happy hymns.
Name it for Tauris, to immortalize
Your flight from home, your rescue from the Furies,
Your penitence and your deliverance.
And let this be the law. When they observe
Her festival, the priest shall hold,
In memory of you, the sharp blade of his knife
Against a human throat and draw one drop
Of blood, then stop—this in no disrespect

But a grave reminder of Her former ways.
Iphigenia! Steps are cut in rock
At Brauron for a shrine to Artemis.
You shall reside as keeper of the keys there
And at your death you shall be buried there
And honored in your tomb with spotless gifts,
Garments unworn, woven by hands of women
Who honorably died in giving birth.
These loyal maidens, Thoas, I command you
To send back home.
Orestes, once I saved you
When I was arbiter on Ares' hill
And broke the tie by voting in your favor.
Now let it be the law that one who earns
An evenly divided verdict wins
His case. Therefore go safely from this land,
O son of Agamemnon. And you, Thoas,
Enjoy the taste of swallowing your wrath.

Thoas

The man who thinks he ever stood a chance
Against the Gods was born a fool. And so
I hold no slightest grievance toward Orestes
Or Iphigenia. They may keep the statue.
There isn't even any dignity
In challenging a God. So off with them.
May Artemis be happy in their land.
I bid these women also, since I have to,
A pleasant trip to Hellas. Thy word holds
For all my captains too. Call back the galleys!
Here are my spirit—and my spear—bowed down.

Athena

In doing as you must, you learn a law
Binding on Gods as well as upon men.
O winds of Heaven, speed Orestes home,

And I will guide him on his way to Athens
And will save Thy likeness, Artemis, my Sister.

The First Maiden

Smooth seas to them and may their journey's end
Become unending joy!

The Fourth Maiden

Pallas Athena, let us prove Thy name
As hallowed upon earth as in high Heaven.

The Third Maiden

And let us take to heart
Thy unexpected but so welcome words.

The Second Maiden

Command us with Thy grace,
O Conqueror of anger and of fear,
Award us wiser ways.

The First Maiden

Undo our troubled guile, crown us with Truth.

HELEN

Translated by Richmond Lattimore

CHARACTERS

Helen

Teucer

Chorus of Greek captive women

Menelaus

Portress

Servant of Menelaus

Theonoë

Theoclymenus

Follower of Theoclymenus

Slave of Theonoë

Castor } *as divine*
Polydeuces }

Because those who are unfamiliar with this play will find that it contains surprises, it is suggested that they read the text first and the introduction afterwards. The introduction is accordingly printed after the play.

HELEN

SCENE: *Egypt, near the Canobic mouth of the Nile and before the gates of the royal house. The tomb of King Proteus is down stage. Helen discovered sitting against the tomb.*

Helen

These are the waters of the Nile, stream of sweet nymphs.
The river, fed with melting of pale snows, and not
with rain, rises to flood the flats of Egypt. Here
Proteus, while yet he lived, was lord over the land,
at home in Pharos, king in Egypt; and his bride
was Psamathe, one of the daughters of the deep,
wife once to Aeacus, later sundered from him,
who bore two children to him in the house, a boy
called Theoclymenus (because his father showed
the gods love in his lifetime) and a fine girl they named
Ido (her mother's image) when she was a child;
but when she came to nubile age they changed her name
to Theonoë, for she understands all things that are,
all things to be, that divination alone can tell.
Nereus, her forefather, granted her this privilege.

Nor is my own country obscure. It is a place
called Sparta, and my father was Tyndareus: though
they tell a story about how Zeus took on himself
the shape of a flying swan, with eagle in pursuit,
and came on wings to Leda my mother, and so won
the act of love by treachery. It may be so.
They called me Helen. Let me tell you all the truth
of what has happened to me. The three goddesses came
to remote Ida, and to Paris, for him to judge
their loveliness, and beauty was the cause. These were
Hera, the Lady of Cyprus, and the Daughter of Zeus.
But Aphrodite, promising my loveliness

(if what is cursed is ever lovely) to the arms
of Paris, won her way. Idaean Paris left
his herds for Sparta, thinking I was to be his.

But Hera, angry that she was not given the prize,
made void the love that might have been for Paris and me
and gave him, not me, but in my likeness fashioning
a breathing image out of the sky's air, bestowed
this on King Priam's son, who thinks he holds me now
but holds a vanity which is not I. See, next,
how further counsels of Zeus add to my misery.
He loaded war upon the Hellenic land and on
the unhappy Phrygians, thus to drain our mother earth
of the burden and the multitude of human kind.
Also, he would advertise the greatest Hellene prince.
The Phrygians fought for me (except it was not I
but my name only) held against the spears of Greece.
I myself was caught up by Hermes, sheathed away
in films of air, for Zeus had not forgotten me,
and set down by him where you see me, in the house
of Proteus, chosen because, most temperate of men,
he could guard my honor safe for Menelaus. So
here am I; but meanwhile my ill-adventured lord
assembled an armament to track me down the trail
of my abduction, and assaulted Ilium's towers.
Because of me, beside the waters of Scamander, lives
were lost in numbers; and the ever patient I
am cursed by all and thought to have betrayed my lord
and for the Hellenes lit the flame of a great war.

Why do I go on living, then? Yet I have heard
from the god Hermes that I yet shall make my home
in the famous plain of Sparta with my lord, and he
shall know I never went to Ilium, had no thought
of bed with any man. Here, while yet Proteus looked
upon this sun we see, I was safe from marriage. Now

that he is dead and hidden in the dark, his son
pursues me for my hand, but I, remembering
my first husband, cling a suppliant here upon
the grave of Proteus, for help to keep my love intact.
Thus, though I wear the name of guilt in Greece, yet here
I keep my body uncontaminated by disgrace.

(Enter Teucer, who does not at first see Helen.)

Teucer

What master holds dominion in these lowering halls?
The scope of wall is royal, and the massive pile
bespeaks possession by the Lord of Gold and Death.
(seeing Helen) Ah!
O gods, what do I see before me. Do I see
the deadly likeness of that woman who destroyed
all the Achaeans and me? May the gods spurn you for
looking so much like Helen's copy. Were I not
footfast on alien ground, with my true-winging shaft
I would have killed you, for looking like the child of Zeus.

Helen

Poor wretch, whoever you are, whatever cause has driven
you here, why must *her* sorrows turn your hate on *me?*

Teucer

I was wrong so to give way to anger more
than it became me. Hellas hates the child of Zeus.
Therefore forgive me, lady, for what I have said.

Helen

But who are you? From what country have you journeyed here?

Teucer

Lady, I am one of those Greek unfortunates.

Helen

It is no wonder you hate Helen then. But tell
me who you are. Where from? Whose son you should be called.

Teucer

My name is Teucer, and the father who gave me life
is Telamon. The land of Salamis nursed my youth.

Helen

And what has brought you to this valley of the Nile?

Teucer

I am an exile, driven from my father's land.

Helen

You must be unhappy. Who was it who forced you out?

Teucer

Telamon, my father. Who could be nearer to my love?

Helen

But why? Such action means catastrophe for you.

Teucer

Aias my brother died at Troy. This meant my doom.

Helen

Surely it was not by your hand he lost his life?

Teucer

His death came when he hurled himself on his own sword.

Helen

In frenzy? Could a sane man see such an act through?

Teucer

You have heard of one they call Achilles, Peleus' son.

Helen

Yes.
He came once to ask for Helen's hand; so we are told.

Teucer

He was killed. His armor caused a quarrel among his friends.

Helen

But how could all this have brought Aias any harm?

Teucer

Someone else won the armor, and he killed himself.

Helen

But has this suffering of his damaged your life?

Teucer

Yes, if only because I did not die with him.

Helen

I see. Tell me, were you at famous Ilium, then?

Teucer

I helped sack it. That act has been my own ruin.

Helen

And the city has been set afire? It is all gone?

Teucer

You could no longer tell for sure where the walls stood.

Helen

Helen, poor wretch! The Phrygians have perished for your sake.

Teucer

The Achaeans also; for great evil has been done.

Helen

How long is it now since the city was destroyed?

Teucer

Seven years have almost circled with their crops since then.

Helen

How much time in addition did you spend at Troy?

Teucer

Moon after moon, until it came to ten full years.

Helen

And then you got the woman of Sparta?

Teucer

Yes we did.

Menelaus seized her by the hair and dragged her off.

Helen

Did you see the poor woman, or have you only heard?

Teucer

I saw her with my own eyes, as I see you now.

Helen

Think. Could this be only an impression, caused by God?

Teucer

Speak of some other matter, please. No more of her.

Helen

You *do* believe your impression is infallible.

Teucer

These eyes saw her. When the eyes see, the brain sees too.

Helen

So. Then by now Menelaus and his wife are home.

Teucer

They are not in Argos, nor where the Eurotas runs.

Helen

You speak them evil, and, ah, you tell of evil for them.

Teucer

The rumor is that he has vanished with his wife.

Helen

Then all the Argives did not cross for home together?

Teucer

They did, but a storm split them and drove them variously.

Helen

Among what waves, where on the open sea?

Teucer

Just as
they cut across the middle of the Aegean main.

Helen

And after this, none knows of Menelaus' return?

Teucer

No one does; and in Greece he is reported dead.

Helen

Then I am undone.

Is Thestius' daughter still alive?

Teucer

You mean by this Leda? No, she is dead and gone.

Helen

It could not have been the shame of Helen that caused her death?

Teucer

They say so; that she fastened the noose on her fair throat.

Helen

Tyndareus' sons, then; are they alive, or are they not?

Teucer

Dead, not dead. There are two interpretations here.

Helen

Which one prevails? How much sorrow must I endure?

Teucer

Men say that they have been made stars and are divine.

Helen

Fair told when thus told; but what is the other account?

Teucer

That for their sister's shame they died by their own hands.
Enough words now. I should not have to suffer twice.
But for the matter of my errand to this house
of kings, it was my wish to see Theonoë
the prophetess. Be you my representative
and help me learn from her how I should steer the wings
of my ship with best wind for the sea-girt land

of Cyprus, where Apollo prophesied that I
should found and name New Salamis from my island home.

Helen

Sail, friend. Your course will show itself; but you must leave
this country and escape before you have been seen
by the son of Proteus, ruler of this land. He now
has gone with hounds, hopeful of killing beasts of chase.
He slaughters every Greek he lays his hands upon,
but why he does this, you must not try to find out,
as I am silent. For how could my speech help you?

Teucer

All you have said was good, my lady, and may the gods
grant you the grace your kindness has deserved. You wear
the bodily shape of Helen, but you have a heart
that is not hers. Wide is the difference. May she
die miserably, never see Eurotas' stream
again.
But may you, lady, always prosper well.

(*Exit. Helen is left alone.*)

Helen

Here, with a song of deep wretchedness for the depth of my sorrows,
what shall be the strain of my threnody, what singing spirit
supplicate in tears, in mourning, in sorrow? Ah me.
You who go winged women in form
young and maiden, daughters of earth,
O Sirens, if you would only come
to attend my mourning
with Libyan harp, with pipes,
with lyres, with tears of your own to give
the singing of all my unhappiness.
With passion for passion, sorrow for sorrow,
melody matching
my dirges, given
by Persephone

of the dead, she in turn shall be given
in her halls of night the sweet of my sorrow
in consecration
of those who are dead and gone from us.

(*Enter the Chorus, singing.*)

Chorus

I was down by the shining blue
water, and on the curl of the grass
there in the golden glare of the sun
laid out the colored wash
in the bed of the young rushes
to dry. There I heard my lady
and the pitiful sound as she cried out,
the voice of sorrow, lament without lyres,
a sharp voice of pain, of mourning
as cries aloud for grief some nymph,
a naiad, caught
in the hills for all her flight, gives voice
to pain, as under the rock hollows
she cries out
on Pan and his captured marriage.

Helen

Hear me,
spoil of the savage oar blade,
daughters of Greece, hear;
from Achaea a mariner
came, yes came, and tears on my tears he loaded.
The wrecked city of Ilium
is given up to the teeth of fire,
all through me and the deaths I caused,
all for my name of affliction. So
Leda has taken her life within
the strangling noose, for the thought of shame
in those sorrows that have been mine.
My lord is lost, he is gone, far driven

over the sea. And the twin-born glory
of the house of my father, Castor
and Polydeuces his brother, vanished,
vanished away; the plain where their horses
trampled, their running-field, desolate
down by the reeds of Eurotas
where the young men rode and ran.

Chorus

Ah me,
so sorrowful was that destiny,
lady mine, that befell you,
a life better unlived
given to you, yes given, when Zeus blazed in the bright
air, in the snowflash of the swan's
wing to beget you upon your mother.
What grief is there you have not known?
What in life have you not lived through?
Your mother is lost and gone:
the twins, beloved children of Zeus,
are blessed in fortune no longer. Your eyes
are kept from the sight of your country,
while through the cities of men there goes
the rumor, divine lady, that gives
you up to barbarian lusts. And now
your husband, lost on the tossing sea,
is gone from life. You can come no more
to bless the halls of your father, bless
the brazen house of Athene.

Helen

What man of the Phrygians was it
or was it one from Hellenic soil
who cut down the dripping pine timbers
fatal to Ilium?
This was the timber that Priam's son
shaped into that accursed ship

which, driven by outland oars, brought him
to the hearth where I lived; he came
after my ill-starred beauty,
after my love's capture.
And she, the treacherous goddess,
the murderous queen of Cyprus,
drew death down on the Danaid men
cruel in all her working.
Then Hera, goddess of grandeur,
queen of the golden throne, who lies
in the arms of Zeus, sent down to me
Hermes, fleet son of Maia.
I was picking fresh flowers
gathering them into my robe, to take
to Athene there in her brazen house
when he caught me away through the bright
air to this unprofitable
country, poor me, made a prize of war
for Priam's sons and the Hellenes
while upon my name
where Simois runs has descended
a false fame and a vanity.

Chorus

You have your sorrows, I know it well. But it were best
to bear your life's constraints as lightly as you may.

Helen

Women and friends, what is this destiny on which
I am fastened? Was I born a monster among mankind?
[No woman, neither in Greece nor yet in Barbary,
is hatched from the white envelope that contains young birds,
yet thus Leda bore me to Zeus, or so they say.]
And so my life is monstrous, and the things that happen
to me, through Hera, or my beauty is to blame.
I wish that like a picture I had been rubbed out
and done again, made plain, without this loveliness,

for so the Greeks would never have been aware of all
those misfortunes that now are mine. So I would keep
what was not bad, as now they keep the bad of me.
He who sees from the gods a single strain of luck,
all bad, has a sad lot, but can endure it still.
More complex is the sorrow in which I am involved.
I have done nothing wrong and yet my reputation
is bad, and worse than a true evil is it to bear
the burden of faults that are not truly yours. Again,
the gods have torn me from my father's land and made
me live among barbarians. I have no kin
and therefore live a slave although my birth was free.
All Barbary is slave except a single man.
There was one anchor to my hope; the thought of how
my husband might come some day and deliver me,
but gone is that hope now, for he is dead and gone.
My mother is dead, I am her murderer. I know
that is unfair, but such unfairness I must take.
My daughter, pride of the household and my own pride,
is growing to gray years unmarried. And the sons
of Zeus, or so men call them, the Dioscuri,
no longer live. So all my luck is turned to grief
and for all purposes I am dead, yet live in fact.
But worst of all is, if I ever should win home
I must be crushed by scandal, for men think that I
am that Helen whom Menelaus went to Troy
to bring. If my husband were alive, I could be known
by him through signs which no one else could recognize.
But this fails now. It cannot be that he lives still.
Why do I go on living then? What course is left?
Shall I choose marriage as my means to get away
from hardship? Live with a barbarian husband? Sit
to a rich table? No, for when a hateful lord
lives with a wife, then all the body is hateful too.
Death is best. But to die in some unseemly way?
[When one hangs by the neck, it is ugly

and is thought a bad sight for the slaves to look upon.
Death by the knife is noble and has dignity
and the body's change from life to death is a short time.]
Such is the depth of my unhappiness, that while
for other women beauty means their happiness
it is my very beauty that has ruined me.

Chorus

Helen, you should not be so sure that that stranger
who came, whoever he is, has spoken all the truth.

Helen

But he said plainly that my husband had been lost.

Chorus

Many things can be said and yet prove to be false.

Helen

And much that contradicts the critic may be true.

Chorus

You push yourself to believe the worst and not the best.

Helen

Yes, I am frightened, and so led by fright to fear.

Chorus

How does your favor stand with those inside the house?

Helen

All here are friends, except the man who hunts my love.

Chorus

Do you know? I think you should . . . leave your place at the tomb. . . .

Helen

What advice is it you so hesitantly give?

Chorus

Go to the house, and ask the daughter of the sea's
nymph, ask Theonoë, who understands all things,

about your husband, whether he still lives, or if
he is lost from daylight. Then, when you are well informed
be happy, or be sorry, as the chance deserves.
Now, when you really know nothing, where is the use
in hurting yourself as you do now? Do what I say.
Give up the shelter of this tomb. Speak with the girl.
Why look further, when in this very house you have
a source of knowledge that will tell you all the truth?
I volunteer to go inside the house with you
and help you ask the maiden for her prophecies.
It is right for women to stand by a woman's cause.

Helen

Friends, I accept your argument.
Go, then, go inside the house
so that there you may ask
what new trials await me now.

Chorus

I will, nor hesitate. Urge not.

Helen

O pitiful day.
Unhappy I, unhappy, oh what
tale of tears shall I be told?

Chorus

Do not be prophetic of grief.
Do not, dear, anticipate sorrow.

Helen

My poor husband, what has happened to him?
Do his eyes see the light,
the sun's chariot and four horses, the stars in course,
or among dead men under ground
takes he the long period?

Chorus

For the future which is yet
to come, lean to the better hope.

Helen

I call upon you by name, I invoke,
river pale by the washed reeds,
Eurotas; if this tale
of my lord's death that has come to me
is true—and where was the story not clear?—
then I will bind my throat
fast in the hanging noose of death,
or with the deadly stroke that cuts
the throat open and bleeding
drive the iron with my own hand hard into my body,
a sacrifice to the trinity
of goddesses, and to Priam's son
who held the hollows of Ida
long ago when he tended his herds.

Chorus

From somewhere may defense emerge
against evils: the turn of your fortune.

Helen

Ah, Troy, the unhappy,
for things done that were never done
you died, hurt pitifully. The gifts
the Lady of Cyprus gave me brought
showers of tears, showers of blood, pain
on pain, tears upon tears, suffering.
Mothers who saw their children die,
maidens who cut their long hair
for kinsmen who were killed beside the waters
of Phrygian Scamander.
Hellas too has cried, has cried
aloud in lamentation,
beaten her hands against her head
and with the nails' track of blood
torn her cheeks' softness.

Blessed long ago in Arcadia, maiden Callisto,
who shared the bed of Zeus, who were made into
a four-foot beast, how happy was your lot beside
my mother's; for all the bear's shaggy bulk
is made gentle by the soft eyes,
and the metamorphosis took away
your sorrows. Artemis drove from her dances
the doe of the golden horns, Titanian daughter of Merops,
for her loveliness. But my body's beauty
ruined the castle of the Dardanians, ruined
all the perished Achaeans.

(*Exeunt all into the house. Enter Menelaus, in tattered clothing.*)

Menelaus

Ah Pelops, racer of chariots and horses long
ago with Oinomäus in the Pisa field,
how I could wish that, when you were constrained to make
an offering to the gods, you had then left this life
for theirs, before you had sired my father, Atreus;
who by his marriage with Aërope begot
Agamemnon and myself, Menelaus, two renowned
brothers; for here I do not boast, yet I believe
we marshalled the greatest of armadas against Troy
although we led them not as tyrants, not by force,
but the young men of Greece willingly served with us.
Those who are no more living can be numbered now,
and those who, gratefully escaping from the sea,
brought home again the names of all the dead. But I,
battered and driven over the gray swell of the open
sea, have been wandering ever since I stormed the towers
of Ilium, trying to win back to my own land
whereto the gods debar my right of homecoming.
I have now sailed to all the friendless, desolate
approaches of Libya; always, as I make near home,
the wind buffets me back again, nor ever fills
favorable my sail to bring me home again.

And now, hapless and shipwrecked, with my friends all lost,
I am driven upon this shore. My ship shattered against
the rocks, and broke up into wreck and flotsam there.
Of all the ship's various parts the keel held out,
and on it, by some unexpected chance, I managed
to save myself and Helen, whom I seized from Troy.
What this land is I do not know, nor yet the name
of its people; I was too embarrassed to be seen
in public, could not ask, but tried to hide away
my ragged state in shame for my bad luck. For when
a great man falls upon evil chance, the strangeness of it
makes him feel worse than the man accustomed to hard times.
But the need is too much for me, for we have no food
nor any clothing for our skin, as you may guess
by the kind of ship's flotsam in which I wrap myself.
The robes and all the shining wraps I had before
are lost at sea with all my treasures. Deep inside
a cave I hid the wife who was the cause of all
my evil fortunes, and constrained those friends who still
are left alive, to keep her safe for me. So now
I am here, all by myself, to see if I can raise
some provisions to take to the friends I left behind.
I saw this house with its expanse of masonry
and the grand gates as of some fortunate man, and so
came here. Seafarers always hope for charity
from the houses of the rich. Those who themselves are poor
would not be able to help them, though the wish were there.
O-ay! Who is the porter here? Will he come out
and take the message of my griefs to those inside?

(*Enter Portress, from the house.*)

Portress

Who is at the gates? Go away, will you, from the house?
Do not keep standing here before the courtyard doors
and bothering the masters. It will mean your death.
You are a Greek, and Greeks are not allowed in here.

Menelaus

Quite so, granny, just as you say, and fair enough.
Very well, I will do what you say, only let me talk.

Portress

Out with you. I have orders, stranger, never to let
anyone come from Greece to stay around this house.

Menelaus

Ah! Keep your hands off me, and stop pushing me.

Portress

That is your fault. You are not doing what I say.

Menelaus

Now go inside and take this message to your master.

Portress

I shall smart for it if I take a message from you.

Menelaus

I am a shipwrecked foreigner of high degree.

Portress

Go on then to some other house instead of this.

Menelaus

No, I am going in; do as I tell you to.

Portress

I tell you, you are bothersome. We'll throw you out.

Menelaus

Ah, where are all my armies now, which won such fame?

Portress

You may have been a great man at home. You are not one here.

Menelaus

God, what a loss of station, and now undeserved.

Portress

Your eyes are wet with tears. Tell me, why are you sad?

Menelaus

Thinking of all my happiness in times gone by.

Portress

Go then, bestow those tears upon your own people.

Menelaus

Tell me first, what is this country, what king's house is this?

Portress

This is the house of Proteus; Egypt is the land.

Menelaus

Egypt? What an unhappy chance to have sailed here.

Portress

What do you find wrong with the glories of the Nile?

Menelaus

Nothing wrong. It is my own bad luck that makes me sad.

Portress

There are many men who have bad luck, not only you.

Menelaus

Is there some master of the house you could name to me?

Portress

This is his tomb you see here. Now his son is king.

Menelaus

Where would he be then? In the house, or gone somewhere?

Portress

He is not in; and above all else he hates Hellenes.

Menelaus

What have we done to him that I should suffer for it?

Portress

It is because Zeus' daughter, Helen, is in this house.

Menelaus

What? What is this you are telling me? Say it again.

Portress

I mean Tyndareus' daughter who lived in Sparta once.

Menelaus

Where did she come from? What is the explanation of this?

Portress

She came from Lacedaemon and made her way here.

Menelaus

When? Has my wife I left in the cave been carried off?

Portress

She came, friend, before the Achaeans sailed for Troy.
So go away from here quietly. The state of things
inside is such that all the great house is upside down.
You came at the wrong time, and if my master catches
you, all the hospitality you will find is death.
I myself like the Greeks, in spite of those harsh words
I gave you. I was afraid of what the master might do.

(*The Portress goes back into the house and closes the door.*)

Menelaus

What am I to think or make of this? She tells me now
of present difficulties grown from those gone by,
since, while I come bringing my wife, lost once by force,
from Troy, and she is guarded for me in the cave,
all the while some other woman with the same name
as my wife has been living in this house. She said
that this one was by birth the child of Zeus. Can it be
there is some man who bears the name of Zeus and lives
beside the banks of the Nile? There is one Zeus; in heaven.
And where on earth is Sparta except only where
Eurotas' waters ripple by the lovely reeds?
Tyndareus is a famous name. There is only one.
And where is there another land called Lacedaemon
or Troy either? I do not know what to make of it.
I suppose it must be that in the great world a great many
have the same name, men named like other men, cities

like cities, women like women. Nothing to wonder at
in this.
I will not run away for the servant's threats.
There is no man whose heart is so uncivilized
that when he has heard my name he will not give me food.
Troy is renowned, and I, who lit the fire of Troy,
Menelaus, am not unknown anywhere in all
the world. I will wait the master of the house. I have
a choice of courses. If he is a savage man
I will hide myself and make for where I left the wreck,
but if he gives way and is gentle, I shall ask
for what the present circumstances make me need.
Of all the evils in my distressed plight, this is
the worst, that I, myself a king, should have to ask
other kings for sustenance. But so it has to be.
For the saying is not mine, but it was wisely said,
that nothing has more strength than dire necessity.

(*Enter the Chorus and Helen from the house.*)

Chorus

Before I came back I heard from the maid
prophetic all she divined for the house
of kings: how Menelaus is not
lost yet nor sunk in the dim,
shining cave of the under-earth,
but still over the sea's surges
hard driven he cannot win
to the harbors of his own land,
in hardship, wandering
for want of food, with his friends all gone
all across the wide world he keeps
his foot hard for the oarsman's stroke
since ever he sailed from Troy land.

Helen

So, here am I, come back to the shelter of the tomb
once more. I have heard Theonoë's words, and they were good,

and she knows everything. She says my husband lives
still in the light and looks upon the day-star; yet
he is driven sailing back and forth along the sea
on endless crossings, hardened by the wanderer's life,
but when his work is ended and over, he will come.
One thing she did not tell me, whether when he comes
he will be safe. I carefully did not ask her this,
I was so happy to hear that he is safe so far.
She said also that he was in this country, near
at hand, a shipwrecked castaway with few friends left.
When will you come? And if you come, how dear to me!

(As she speaks this line, she turns to face Menelaus, whom she has not seen until now. She gives a little scream.)

Who is it, who are you? Does this mean I am waylaid
by the machinations of Proteus' godless son? What shall
I do? Not run like a racing filly, like the god's
bacchanal, to the tomb with flying feet? This man
is savage by his look and hunts me for his prey.

Menelaus

You, who now race in such an agony of fear
to reach the grave-mound and the uprights where the fires
are burned, stay! Why this flight? Know, when I saw your face
it struck me with amazement and with unbelief.

Helen

We are set upon, my women. This man bars my way
to the tomb. His purpose is to catch me, and then give
me over to that tyrant whose embrace I shun.

Menelaus

I am no thief, nor any servant of bad men.

Helen

And yet the clothes that cover you are poor and mean.

Menelaus

Stay your swift feet from running, put aside your fear.

Helen

Very well, I will stand, since I have reached my goal.

Menelaus

Who are you? I look, lady, upon your face: whose face?

Helen

And who are you? The same question for both of us.

Menelaus

Never have I seen a form so like another form.

Helen

Oh gods!—it is divine to recognize your own.

Menelaus

Are you a Hellene woman or a native here?*

Helen

Hellene. But tell me who you are. I would know too.

Menelaus

You are more like Helen, my lady, than any I know.

Helen

You are like Menelaus, too. What does it mean?

Menelaus

The truth. You have recognized that most unhappy man.

Helen

Oh, you are come at long last here to your wife's arms.

Menelaus

Wife? What wife do you mean? Take your hands off my clothes.

Helen

The wife Tyndareus, my own father, gave to you.

Menelaus

O Hecate of the lights, send better dreams than this.

* The line is not in the manuscripts of this play. Markland has supplied it from the parody of this scene in Aristophanes' *Thesmophoriazusae*.

Helen

I am no dream of the crossway goddess. You see me.

Menelaus

I am only one man and could not have two wives.

Helen

And who might be this other mate whose lord you are?

Menelaus

Whom the cave hides, whom I brought here from the Phrygian land.

Helen

I am your wife. There is no other in my place.

Menelaus

Am I in my right senses? Are my eyes at fault?

Helen

When you look at me, do you not think you see your wife?

Menelaus

Your body is like her. Certainty fails me.

Helen

Look and see.
What more do you want? And who knows me better than you?

Menelaus

In very truth you are like her. That I will not deny.

Helen

What better teacher shall you have than your own eyes?

Menelaus

It is they that fail me, since another is my wife.

Helen

It was an image of me. I never went to Troy.

Menelaus

And what artificer makes bodies live and breathe?

Helen
The air: from which the work of gods shaped you a bride.

Menelaus
And which of the gods made her? This is past all wit.

Helen
Hera, to palm on Paris, so he should not have me.

Menelaus
How could you be here and in Troy at the same time?

Helen
My name could be in many places where I was not.

Menelaus
Let me go. I had pain enough when I came here.

Helen
And will you leave me, for that empty shadow's arms?

Menelaus
You are like Helen, so, at least, happy farewell.

Helen
Lost, lost! I won my husband, and must lose him still.

Menelaus
I trust my memory of great hardships more than you.

Helen
Ah me, was any woman more wretched ever? They
who stand closest forsake me. I shall never find
my way to Greece, land of my fathers, ever again.

(*Enter Servant of Menelaus. He does not see, or does not notice, Helen until he has told his story.*)

Servant
Menelaus, I have been wandering all over this land
of barbarians looking for you and find you now
at last. The friends you left behind sent me for you.

Menelaus

What is it? Have the barbarians robbed or plundered you?

Servant

A strange thing, stranger in itself than the telling of it.

Menelaus

Tell me. You must bring some surprise, for haste like this.

Servant

I tell you: all your thousand toils were toiled in vain.

Menelaus

This is old weeping for old sorrows. What is new?

Servant

Your wife is gone, swept up and away and out of sight
into the hollows of the high air. Sky veils her now.
She left the secret cave where we were keeping her
with only this said to us: "Wretched men of Troy
and all you Achaeans who, day after day, went on
dying for me beside Scamander, by Hera's craft,
you thought Paris had Helen, when he never did.
Now I, having kept the duty of destiny, stayed out
the time I had to stay, go back into the sky,
my father. All for nothing Tyndareus' daughter has
heard evil things said of her, who did nothing wrong."
Oh, daughter of Leda, hail! Were you here all this time?
I was in the act of telling him, fool that I was,
how you had left our caverns for the stars and gone
on wings away. I will not let you mock at us
like this again. It was enough hardship that you,
your husband, and his helpers gave us there in Troy.

Menelaus

I see it, I see it! All the story that she told
has come out true. O day of my desires, that gave
you back into my arms to take and hold again!

Helen

Oh, dearest of men to me, Menelaus, time has grown
old, but the joy that now is ours is fresh and new.
I have my husband again, all my delight, sweet friends,
my arms circle him now,
beloved, light and a flame in dark that has been so long.

Menelaus

And I hold you. And we have so much to say about
the time between, I do not know where to begin.

Helen

I am so happy, all my hair is rising
with shivering pleasure, and the tears burst. Husband
and love, I have your body here close in my arms,
happiness, mine again.

Menelaus

O sweetest face, there is nothing left to wish for.
This is my bride, daughter of Zeus and Leda,
she whom the maidens of white horses, girls of your kindred
brought me by candle-light, to bless me, to bless
me long ago, but it was a god who took you away
from my house, and drove you
away, where your fate was the stronger.
But evil turned to good brought us together again,
my wife, lost so long. Now may my luck be good.

Chorus

May it be good, surely. All my prayer is as your prayer.
Where there are two, one cannot be wretched, and one not.

Helen

My friends, dear friends, I will no longer
weep and grieve for the past.
I have my husband, I have him. Long I waited for him,
all the years of Troy, waited for him to come.

Menelaus

You have me, I have you. But the suns of ten thousand days
were hard to win through to God's gladness here at the end.
My happiness has its tears in it; but there is more
sweetness here than the pain.

Helen

What shall I say? Who ever could hope that this would be,
to have you so unhoped-for here against my breasts?

Menelaus

Or I to hold you, when I thought you had gone away
to Idaean Troy and to those pitiful towers.
In gods' name, tell me how you were taken from my house.

Helen

Ah, a bitter cause that you open here,
and ah, a bitter story you waken for me.

Menelaus

Speak. The gods gave this; we must even hear it out.

Helen

I spit away that story, the story that I must tell.

Menelaus

Tell it still. There is pleasure in hardships heard about.

Helen

It was not to the bed of a young barbarian man
borne on the beating of oars,
borne on the beating of desire for a lawless love.

Menelaus

No, but what spirit, what destiny robbed home of you?

Helen

The son of Zeus, of Zeus, my lord,
brought me here to the Nile.

Menelaus

Strange, strange! Who sent him? There is danger in this tale.

Helen

I have wept for this, my eyes are wet with tears.
It was the wife of Zeus destroyed me.

Menelaus

Hera? What need had she to make it evil for us?

Helen

Ah, there was danger for me in the bathing there and the springs
where the goddesses made bright
their bodies; there the judgment was begun.

Menelaus

And Hera made the judgment mean this evil for you?

Helen

So she might take away from Paris. . . .

Menelaus

How? Speak.

Helen

Me. Cypris had promised him me.

Menelaus

Oh, cruel.

Helen

Cruel, cruel. So I was driven to Egypt.

Menelaus

She gave him the image in your place. So you tell me.

Helen

But you in your house, my mother, ah, the sorrows of you,
the hurt that happened.

Menelaus

Tell me.

Helen

My mother is gone. Ill starred in marriage for my sake
and for my shame she caught the noose to her neck.

Menelaus

Ah. But Hermione our daughter, does she live?

Helen

Wedless, childless, my dear, she grieves
for my marriage that was none.

Menelaus

Oh, Paris, you sacked my house from top to bottom, and yet
it killed you too, and in their thousands killed
the bronze armored Danaans.

Helen

It was the god who cast me away from my city, from you,
out of the land of my fathers, star-crossed and cursed
when I left my house, when I left my bed; but I left them not
for any shameful love.

Chorus

If now for the rest of fortune you are fortunate,
in time to come, it is enough to heal the past.

Servant

Menelaus, let me into your happiness as well.
I begin to understand it, but am not yet clear.

Menelaus

Indeed, my father. Share in what we have to say.

Servant

Is she not mistress of sorrows for the men in Troy?

Menelaus

She is not. We were swindled by the gods. We had
our hands upon an idol of the clouds.

Servant

You mean
it was for a cloud, for nothing, we did all that work?

Menelaus

The hand of Hera, the hate of the three goddesses.

Servant

This woman who stands here with us is your real wife?

Menelaus

Herself. It is I who tell you this. You must believe.

Servant

My daughter, the way of God is complex, he is hard
for us to predict. He moves the pieces and they come
somehow into a kind of order. Some have bad luck
while others, scatheless, meet their evil and go down
in turn. None can hold fortune still and make it last.
You and your husband have had your turn of trouble now.
Yours was a story, but he fought with the spear, and all
his hard fighting was fought for nothing. Now his luck
has turned, and the highest blessings fall into his hands.
You never shamed your aged father, never shamed
your divine brothers, nor did what you were rumored to.
It all comes back to me, your marriage long ago,
and I remember the torch I carried as I ran
beside your four-horse chariot, where you, a bride,
rode from your noble house beside the master here.
He is a poor thing who does not feel as his masters do,
grieve in their grief, be happy in their happiness.
I, though I wear the name of lackey, yet aspire
to be counted in the number of the generous
slaves, for I do not have the name of liberty
but have the heart. Better this, than for a single man
to have the double evil of an evil spirit
and to be named by those about him as a slave.

Menelaus

Come then, old friend, you who have had your share of work
in the hard stands beneath the shield and at my side,
share now the blessings of my fortune too, and go
to take the news back to those friends I left behind
how you have found our state here, how our luck holds now;
tell them, too, to wait by the sea-shore, follow from there

the progress of those trials of strength I see in store
for me, and if we can steal my wife out of this place
they must see to it that, joining our fortunes all in one,
we get clear of these natives, if we have the strength.

Servant

It shall be done, my lord.
Only, now I am sure
how rotten this business of prophets is, how full of lies.
There never was any good in burning things on fires
nor in the voices of fowl. It is sheer idiocy
even to think that birds do people any good.
Calchas said nothing about this, he never told
the army when he saw his friends die for a cloud,
nor Helenus either, and a city was stormed in vain.
You might say: "No, for God did not wish it that way."
Then why consult the prophets? We should sacrifice
to the gods, ask them for blessings, and let prophecy go.
The art was invented as a bait for making money,
but no man ever got rich on magic without work.
The best prophet is common sense, our native wit.

(*Exit.*)

Chorus

My own opinion about prophets marches with
that of this old man. If you have the gods for friends
you have a better thing than prophecy in your house.

Helen

So. All has been peaceful here where I have been. But tell
me, my poor husband, how you survived Troy. I know
there is no good in learning, but when you love you feel
a fascination in even the sorrows of those you love.

Menelaus

Your single question, one approach, ask me so much.
Why must I tell you how the Aegean wore us out,
of the Euboean wrecking-fires Nauplius set,

of Crete, of the Libyan cities we were driven upon,
of Perseus' eyrie? I could never satisfy
you telling of troubles. Telling would only burden me
who am so tired already, and be double pain.

Helen

What you have said was better than my question. Still,
leave out the rest and tell me only this. How long
have you been wandering battered on the waves of the sea?

Menelaus

The years at Troy were ten, and to this add the time
I was at sea, where I filled the circles of seven years.

Helen

Too long, unhappy husband, all too long a time
to live through, and survive it, and come here to die.

Menelaus

To die! What will you tell me now? You have broken me.

Helen

Make your escape, get clear of this place with speed, or else
you must be killed by the man who is the master here.

Menelaus

What have I done to deserve treatment such as this?

Helen

You have come unlooked-for to prevent my marrying.

Menelaus

You mean someone here is trying to marry my wife?

Helen

He meant to force my favors; and I must endure.

Menelaus

In his own private strength, or by some lordship here?

Helen

The man is Proteus' son and master of the land.

Menelaus
Now I understand the puzzle of the portress' speech.

Helen
At what outlandish doors have you been standing now?

Menelaus
These. And like any beggar I was driven away.

Helen
You were not asking for charity? Oh, my shame.

Menelaus
The action was that, but I did not call it so.

Helen
It seems, then, you know all about his courting me.

Menelaus
I know; what I do not know is whether you held him off.

Helen
Hear it then: all my love is kept untouched for you.

Menelaus
What will make me sure of this? (but how sweet, if true!).

Helen
Do you see where I sat in suffering beside this tomb?

Menelaus
The marks, yes, of your suffering. What was your plan?

Helen
I took a suppliant's place here to escape his bed.

Menelaus
For lack of an altar, or is it a foreign custom here?

Helen
It saved me, as well as the gods' temples could have done.

Menelaus
Is there no way for me and my ship to take you home?

Helen
A sword waits for you, rather than a love-bed with me.

Menelaus
Thus I would be the most unhappy man alive.

Helen
Take flight, and do not be ashamed. Escape from here.

Menelaus
And leave you? It was for your sake I captured Troy.

Helen
But better so than that my love should mean your death.

Menelaus
Cowardly counsel, unworthy of the siege of Troy.

Helen
You would kill the king, I suspect. It cannot be done.

Menelaus
You mean he has a body that no steel can pierce?

Helen
You will see. The bold are helpless without cleverness.

Menelaus
Shall I then quietly give him my hands to tie?

Helen
You are desperate. What we need now is strategy.

Menelaus
I would rather die in action than die passively.

Helen
There is a single hope for escape, a single way.

Menelaus
What way? Bribery? Daring and force? Or argument?

Helen
What if the tyrant never learns that you are here?

Menelaus
Who will tell him? He will not know me by himself.

Helen
He has an ally, strong as a god, inside the house.

Menelaus
Has Rumor come and taken a secret place inside?

Helen
No, it is his sister, whom they call Theonoë.

Menelaus
The name is ominous, surely. Tell me what she does.

Helen
She knows everything. She will tell her brother you are here.

Menelaus
That would be death. I have no way to lie concealed.

Helen
But if we threw ourselves on her mercy, worked on her?

Menelaus
To do what? What is the hope you lead me gently to?

Helen
That she will *not* tell her brother you are in the land.

Menelaus
If we won her over, could we get ourselves out of here?

Helen
With her help, easily. Without her knowledge, no.

Menelaus
Best for woman to approach woman. You do this.

Helen
She will not leave until my arms have embraced her knees.

Menelaus
But look now. What if she will not listen to us?

Helen

You must die, and I be married by force, and sorrowful.

Menelaus

But treacherous still. By force, you say. Only an excuse.

Helen

No, then. I have sworn a sacred oath, by your own head.

Menelaus

You mean that you will die and never change your mate?

Helen

Die by the sword that kills you, and be laid to rest
beside you.

Menelaus

I accept it. Take my hand on this.

Helen

I take it, swear to forsake the daylight when you die.

Menelaus

And I swear, when I lose you I shall take my life.

Helen

How, in such death, shall we make men know how we died?

Menelaus

I will kill you on this grave-mound, then kill myself.
But come, first we shall dare a great action for your sake
and for your marriage. If he wants you, let him come.
I will not shame my glories of the Trojan War
nor take the common blame of Hellas when I come home,
I who made Thetis lose Achilles, I who looked
on Telamonian Aias in his suicide
and saw Nestor made childless. Shall I then not dare
count death as worth the dying for my lady's sake?
Oh, I must. If there are gods and if they are wise,
when a man falls high-hearted in the close of war
they make the earth lie light upon him in the grave,
but fling the cowards out on the hard stones of earth.

Chorus

Oh gods, I pray you, let the race of Tantalus
turn fortunate at last, and let their troubles end.

Helen

Unhappy me! My destiny is luckless still.
Menelaus, we have no chance left. Theonoë
the diviner is coming out now, for the house sounds
to the unbarring of the doors. Run! Only where
to run? What use? Whether or not she is here, she knows
that you are here. Poor husband, it is ruin now.
Saved from the savages of Troy, you have come here
once again to be driven on a savage sword.

(*Enter Theonoë from the house, attended by women who carry torches and a sacred image. Each of her instructions is to a single attendant.*)

Theonoë

Lead the way. Carry torches, let them shine, and bring
the image, gift of the solemn sky, from its inward room
so we may take and breathe the purity of this air.
You: if anyone with unhallowed foot has stepped
and fouled the way, treat it with purifying flame,
then quench the blaze so I can make my way through. Then
when we have rendered my devotion to the gods
take the fire back inside to burn upon the hearth.

Helen, what of my prophecies? Are they not true?
Here is your husband Menelaus, plain before
my eyes, with his ships lost, and with your image gone.
Poor man, with what dangers escaped you have come here,
nor even yet know whether you shall go home or must
stay here. This very day before the seat of Zeus
there shall be argument among the gods about
your case. Hera, who was your enemy before
is now your friend, desires that you go home with Helen
here, so that Greece may learn how Aphrodite's gift
to Alexander of a bride was a false gift.

Cypris would wreck your homecoming, so none shall know
the truth of how she bought the name of beauty for
false payment, Helen's marriage—which was no real thing.
The decision rests with me, to do as Cypris wills
and tell my brother you are here, destroy you so,
or take the side of Hera, save your life, and hide
your coming from my brother, though his orders were
to tell him, when your journey home brought you this way.

Which of you will go tell my brother that this man
is here? Thus will my future be made safe for me.

(*Helen flings herself at the feet of Theonoë.*)

Helen

Maiden, I throw myself as suppliant against
your knees, and kneel in a forlorn posture, for the sake
of my own self and for this man. I have found him
at last, and finding him am like to see him die.
Do not then tell your brother that my husband here
has come to my most loving and beloved arms,
but save us, I implore you. You must not betray
your duty and your good name for a brother's sake
to buy him wicked pleasures he does not deserve.
God hates violence. He has ordained that all men
fairly possess their property, not seize it. So
the rich man who is wicked must be left in peace.
There is the sky, which is all men's together, there
is the world to live in, fill with houses of our own
nor hold another's, nor tear it from his hands by force.
For me it was hard, and yet it was a blessed thing,
that Hermes gave me to your father to keep safe
for my husband, who is here and who would have me back.
How can he take me back when he is dead? And how
could your father duly give the living to the dead?
Consider now your father's case, the case of God.
Would the divine power, and would the dead man, wish to see
what belongs to another given back, or would they not?

I think they would. You must not give a greater weight
to a wild brother than to an honorable father.
If you, who are a prophetess and lead men through
the ways of God, spoil the just actions of your father
and uphold the right of an unrighteous brother, then
knowing the ways of God is a disgraceful thing.
Shame to know past and future, not know right and wrong!
Save me from my misfortunes, from hardships where I
submit. It is an accidental gift of grace.
There is no man living but Helen is his hate,
notorious through all Hellas as having betrayed
my husband, to live in the golden houses of the East.
But if I go to Greece and reach Sparta again
and they hear, and see, how it was by the arts of gods
that they were ruined, that I never betrayed my loves,
they will restore me to my reputation once
again. My daughter—nobody will take her now—
shall be given by me. I shall escape the shabby life
I lead here, and live on my own money in my own house.
If Menelaus lay dead and murdered on the pyre,
I should have loved him from my distance, with my tears.
But he is here, alive. Must he be taken from me?

No maiden, no. I kneel here as your suppliant.
Give me your grace in this, and let your ways be like
your upright father's ways, for it is the brightest fame
of children, when they have a father who was good,
if they can match the character that gave them birth.

Chorus

The words you have spoken since we spoke are pitiful
and you have pathos too. Yet still, I long to hear
what Menelaus has to argue for his life.

Menelaus

I cannot bring myself to fall before your feet
nor to make my eyes wet with tears. Such abjectness
would be the greatest shame upon the tale of Troy.

Yet I have heard, or read, how even stately men
have found it in them to let tears burst from their eyes.
I waive this privilege of honor—if privilege
of honor it is. Courage is better.
Rather, thus:
if you think best to save a man, an outlander,
who asks with right to have his wife given back to him,
give her, and save me too. If you do not think it best,
it does not mean new misery for me but the old
continued; and it means you are an evil woman.
But what I think is worthy and right for me to say,
and what will take your heart beyond all else, I shall
say here before your father's monument, in grief.

Aged sir, here indwelling in the stony tomb,
give her back to me. What I ask is my own wife
whom Zeus had brought here, so you could keep her safe for me.
I understand now you will never give her back
since you are dead. But she must not deign that the invoked
and so much honored father underground shall hear
despiteful speech against him. All is in her hands.

Hades of the downworld, I invoke your aid as well.
You have taken many dead men, fallen before my sword,
because of this woman. You are paid your price in full.
Now bring these bodies to life again and yield them back,
or force this maiden to outpass her father's fame
for right dealing, and give me back the bride of my love.
If you Egyptians take my wife away from me,
I will tell you what will happen then, as she did not.
For your attention, maiden: we are bound by oath.
First I shall find your brother and we two shall fight.
He will be killed, or I. There is no more to say.
But if he lacks the courage to stand up to me,
and tries to starve and snare two suppliants at the tomb,
I have decided to kill her, then thrust the blade
of this two-edged sword into my own heart, upon

the back of this grave mound before us, where the blood
will splash and drip upon the grave. There we shall lie
two corpses, side by side, upon the marble tomb,
to shame your father, to hurt you, forevermore.
Your brother will not marry her. Nobody else
will marry her. I shall take her away with me,
away to the dead, if I am not to bring her home.

Why do I say this? Turning to woman and to tears
I should be pitied, but I should get nothing done.
Kill me, if you think best. You will not kill your shame.
But better, be persuaded by my arguments;
for so you would be just, and I should have my wife.

Chorus

It is yours to pass judgment on their arguments,
maiden. Judge then, and judge so all will be well pleased.

Theonoë

My nature is to deal fairly; so is my wish.
I have myself to think of, and my father's name
is not to be defiled. I must not give my brother
such pleasures as will leave me with my honor gone.
The sanctity of justice is a powerful thing
in my own nature. This is Nereus' heritage.
I have it, Menelaus; I will try to keep
it always. And, since Hera wishes to help you,
my vote shall be as Hera votes. And as for Love
(may Love not be offended!) that means nothing here.
My aim is to remain a maiden all my life.
As for reproaches on my father and this tomb,
the same tale must apply to me. I should do wrong
not to restore her. For my father, had he lived,
would have given her back to you, and you to her.
For all men, in the world below and in the world
above must pay for acts committed here. The mind
of those who have died, blown into the immortal air,
immortally has knowledge, though all life is gone.

I must not strain this matter to great length. I shall
be quiet about your supplication, and shall not
let my good counsels help my brother toward his lust.
Really, I serve him so, though I seem not to do,
if I can make him good, not dissolute any more.
Now it will rest upon yourselves to find a way.
I shall have nothing to do with it, but shall withdraw
and be silent. Begin by praying to the gods, and ask
the Lady of Cyprus to let Helen now come home,
and ask Hera to hold steadfastly that good will
toward you, and toward your husband, which shall save you both.

My father, you are dead, but while I have the strength
your name of goodness shall not change to a vile name.

(*Exit, attended.*)

Chorus

The unrighteous are never really fortunate.
Our hopes for safety depend upon our doing right.

Helen

We are safe, Menelaus, as far as the maiden is concerned.
Now it is yours to propose measures, so that we
can make a plan between us to escape from here.

Menelaus

Listen then: you have lived some time in this house
and have been familiar with the attendants of the king.

Helen

Yes, but why did you mention it? Does it mean you hope
to accomplish something that will help the two of us?

Menelaus

Would you be able to persuade those who have charge
of the chariots? Would they perhaps give us one?

Helen

I could persuade them. But what course? How shall we run
the plains of this strange land where we do not know our way?

Menelaus

Hopeless, as you say. . . . Come, then, hide me in the house
and I kill the king with my own blade. Shall we do this?

Helen

No. His sister could no longer keep the secret
of your presence here, if it were to mean her brother's death.

Menelaus

But we have no ship in which to make a safe escape.
The ship we had is at the bottom of the sea.

Helen

I know! Even a woman might have one clever thought.
Are you willing, though not dead, to be reported dead?

Menelaus

Unlucky omen. But if it does us any good
I consent. You may say that I am dead, though I am not.

Helen

Then we shall use the pitiful customs of women,
the dirges and cutting of hair to the unhallowed god.

Menelaus

Where is there any help toward our escape in this?
I think there is some trick lurking behind your words.

Helen

Yes. I will say that you have died at sea, and ask
the king to let me bury you in effigy.

Menelaus

Suppose he grants it? Even so, without a ship,
how shall we save our bodies by this funeral?

Helen

I shall ask him for conveyance, so your burial
fineries may be submerged and gathered in the sea's arms.

Menelaus

Well spoken, except for one thing. He will merely say
you must bury him on land. Where, then, is your excuse?

Helen

But I shall tell him that in Greece it is not allowed
to bury ashore those who have met their death at sea.

Menelaus

Right again; so you correct it. Then I too shall sail
in the same boat, and with you let the offerings down.

Helen

By all means, yes, you are to be there. Bring with you
those mariners of yours who escaped from the shipwreck.

Menelaus

Thus once I get possession of the anchored ship
there will be fighting, man to man, sword against sword.

Helen

You shall be in charge of all thenceforward. Only let
the wind blow fair in our sail. Let the ship run!

Menelaus

It shall. The gods will end my troubles now at last.
Who will you say has told you the story of my death?

Helen

You. And you tell him you sailed with Atreus' son, and that
you were the sole survivor, and you saw him die.

Menelaus

This fishing-net of rags I wear upon myself
will be most authentic evidence of my spindrift state.

Helen

It is timely now, though your ship was untimely lost.
The misery of time since might turn now to good.

Menelaus

Should I then go inside the house with you, or sit
here and wait quietly for you beside the tomb?

Helen

Stay here. So, if he uses violence on you
this tomb, and then your own sword, will be your defense.
I shall go in the house and cut my curls and change
the white clothing that I wear for black, and drag
my nails across my cheek leaving a red furrow there.
I must. Great hazard. I see two ways the scales can tip.
I may be caught in treachery, then I must die.
Or I shall save your life, and we shall both go home.
O queen and goddess, given to the arms of Zeus,
Hera. We are two pitiful people. Grant us wind
from work. We ask, and lift our arms straight toward that sky
where your home is, among the splendors of the stars.
And you, whose beauty's cost was my brute marriage, you
Dione's daughter, Cyprian, oh destroy me not.
It is enough, that filth you rolled me in before
when you gave barbarians not my body but my name.
But if you wish to kill me, let me only die
in my own country. Why this thirst for evil things?
Why do you work in passions, lies, devices full
of treachery, love-magics, murder in the home?
Were you only temperate, in all else you are found sweet
to us beyond all other gods. This I confess.

(*Exit into the house.*)

Chorus

To you, who deep forested, choired in the growth
of singing wood hide nested,
to you I utter my outcry,
to you, beyond all other birds sweet in your singing,
O nightingale of the sorrows
come, with brown beak shaken,
to the beat of your melody, come

with song to my sad singing
as I mourn for the hard sorrows
of Helen, for all the suffering,
all the tears of the daughters of Troy
from spears held by Achaeans,
all from the time when with outland oar he swept over
the water-flats, came, came, and his coming was sorrow
in marriage for Priam's people, moving
from Lacedaemon, from you, Helen: Paris, dark lover
brought there by Aphrodite.

And there were many Achaeans who by the spear
and by the stone's smash have died
and are given, in vain, to Hades.
For these, unhappy wives have cut their long hair.
The chambers of their love are left forsaken.
Many Achaeans besides
the man of the single oar drowned
off waterswept Euboea
when he lit his wreck fires, blazed
the false flares, and crashed them to death
on Aegean rocks at Caphereus.
And the harborless mountains of Malea in the storm wind
were death, when he fled from our land, with the prize of his outland
glory; prize, no prize, but war,
the Greek cloud shape his ship carried off,
the divine image of Hera.

What is god, what is not god, what is between man
and god, who shall say? Say he has found
the remote way to the absolute,
that he has seen god, and come
back to us, and returned there, and come
back again, reason's feet leaping
the void? Who can hope for such fortune?
Yourself were born, Helen, daughter to Zeus.

Winged in the curves of Leda there
as bird he childed you.
Yet even you were hallooed through Greece
as traitress, faithless, rightless, godless. No man's
thought I can speak of is ever clear.
The word of god only I found unbroken.

(Helen returns and joins Menelaus.)

Mindless, all of you, who in the strength of spears
and the tearing edge win your valors
by war, thus stupidly trying
to halt the grief of the world.
For if bloody debate shall settle
the issue, never again
shall hate be gone out of the cities of men.
By hate they won the chambers of Priam's city;
they could have solved by reason and words
the quarrel, Helen, for you.
Now these are given to the Death God below.
On the walls the flame, as of Zeus, lightened and fell.
And you, Helen, on your sorrows bear
more hardships still, and more matter for grieving.

(Enter Theoclymenus, from the country, attended by hunters.)

Theoclymenus

Tomb of my father, greeting! It was even for such
addresses, Proteus, I caused you to be buried here
at the entrance, and in passing in and out of doors
I, Father, Theoclymenus your son, greet you.

You, my serving men, take the dogs and the hunting-nets
inside the king's palace, put them away.
Now I
have found many hard things to say against myself.
Do we not chastise evildoers with death? And yet
even now they tell me there has been a Greek man seen
who has openly come here but has escaped the guards,

to spy on us, or watching for the chance to steal
Helen away. Let him be caught, and he is dead.
Ah,
I have come too late, it seems. The whole thing has been done
and the daughter of Tyndareus, leaving empty her place
in the tomb's shelter, is carried away out of the land.
Hallo! Unbar all bolts and let the horses out
from their mangers, men, and get the chariots out and ready.
Let it not be for lack of effort that the bride
I would win is stolen secretly from my domain.

No, wait. I see the two that I am after, here
beside the palace still, they have not yet escaped.
Why have you changed from your white clothes, and put on black
and wear them? Why have you put the iron to your head
and shorn away the glory of your lovely hair?
And why are your cheeks wet with the fresh tears? For whom
do you weep? Is it compulsion of dreams in the night
that makes you sorrow so, or have you heard from home
some rumor, and the grief of it has wrecked your heart?

Helen

My lord—for now at last I name you in such terms—
my life is ruined. There is nothing left for me.

Theoclymenus

What has happened? What is the disaster that has struck you down?

Helen

My Menelaus—how shall I say it? He is dead.

Theocylmenus

I cannot take pleasure in what you tell me, though it is
my fortune. How do you know? Did Theonoë tell you?

Helen

She says so. Also, one who was with him when he died.

Theoclymenus
There is someone here then, with an authentic report?

Helen
Yes, here. May he go where I too desire to go.

Theoclymenus
Who is he? Where is he? Tell me, let me get this clear.

Helen
That man you see there, sitting abject under the tomb.

Theoclymenus
By Apollo! The rags of clothing he is in!

Helen
I think my husband has looked thus. I pity both.

Theoclymenus
Who is this man? Where from? Where did he come ashore?

Helen
He is a Greek, an Achaean who sailed with my husband.

Theoclymenus
What manner of death does he say that Menelaus died?

Helen
The most pitiful; washed down in the running sea.

Theoclymenus
Where in our remote waters was he sailing then?

Helen
He was driven against Libya's harborless cliffs.

Theoclymenus
How was this man his oarsmate, and yet did not die?

Helen
Sometimes the baser have more fortune than their betters.

Theoclymenus
He is here, a castaway. Where did he leave his ship?

Helen

Where I wish he had perished, and Menelaus had not.

Theoclymenus

But Menelaus has perished. In what boat did he come?

Helen

Sailors came on him and picked him up, or so he says.

Theoclymenus

Where is that evil that was brought to Troy instead of you?

Helen

The cloud image? You mean that? Gone into the sky.

Theoclymenus

O Priam, O Troy, how you were brought down in vain!

Helen

I too, with Priam's children, shared this luckless chance.

Theoclymenus

Did he leave your husband unburied? Is he beneath ground?

Helen

Not buried yet. And oh, my grief!

Theoclymenus

Was it for this
you cut away the long curls of your yellow hair?

Helen

He is dear to me. Whoever is with me now is dear.

Theoclymenus

This is real. Sorrow has distracted her to tears.

Helen

It could easily happen that your own sister might die.

Theoclymenus

Oh, no. How?
Will you go on making this tomb your home?

Helen

Why do you make fun of me? Let the dead man be.

Theoclymenus

Yet you showed faith to him when you avoided me.

Helen

That is all past. You may make the wedding arrangements now.

Theoclymenus

It has been long in coming, but I still am glad.

Helen

Do you know what we should do? Let us forget the past.

Theoclymenus

What terms? Grace should be given in return for grace.

Helen

Let us make peace between ourselves. Forgive me all.

Theoclymenus

My quarrel with you is cancelled. Let it go with the wind.

Helen

But by your knees I ask of you, if you are my friend—

Theoclymenus

What is it that your suppliant arms would wrest from me?

Helen

I desire your permission to bury my dead lord.

Theoclymenus

How? Are there graves for the lost? Would you bury a shadow?

Helen

There is a Greek custom for those who die at sea.

Theoclymenus

What is it? Pelops' people are knowing in such things.

Helen

To hold a burial ceremony in empty robes.

Theoclymenus

Do it, then. Raise a mound on my land, where you wish.

Helen

It is not thus we bury our drowned mariners.

Theoclymenus

How, then? I cannot keep up with Greek usages.

Helen

We take all the dead should be given out to sea.

Theoclymenus

What shall I give you for your dead, then?

Helen

This man knows.

I am inexperienced. All my luck was good before.

Theoclymenus

So, friend, you have brought me news that I am glad to hear.

Menelaus

Not good hearing for me, nor for the dead.

Theoclymenus

Tell me,

how do you bury those who have been drowned at sea?

Menelaus

As lavishly as a man's substance lets him do.

Theoclymenus

For this woman's sake tell me without minding the cost.

Menelaus

First, there must be a blood-victim for the undergods.

Theoclymenus

What beast? Only tell me, and I will do your will.

Menelaus

Decide yourself. Whatever you give will satisfy.

Theoclymenus

Among us outlanders, it would be a bull or horse.

Menelaus

Give such then, only give nothing which is malformed.

Theoclymenus

Our herds are rich. We have no lack of good victims.

Menelaus

Coverings are given too for the body, though none is there.

Theoclymenus

That will be done. Is anything else customary?

Menelaus

Brazen armor; for Menelaus loved the spear.

Theoclymenus

What we shall give will be worthy of Pelops' clan.

Menelaus

We need also other fair produce of the earth.

Theoclymenus

What will you do? How will you sink all this in the sea?

Menelaus

A ship must be there, also rowers to man the oars.

Theoclymenus

How far distant is the ship to be from the land?

Menelaus

Out where the breakers can barely be seen from ashore.

Theoclymenus

Tell me, why does Greece keep this custom? For what cause?

Menelaus

So the waves cannot wash pollution back ashore.

Theoclymenus

You shall have a fast-running Phoenician ship, with oars.

Menelaus

That would be excellent. Menelaus would like it so.

Theoclymenus

Do you need her too? Can you not do it by yourself?

Menelaus

A man's mother must do this, or his wife, or children.

Theoclymenus

You mean it is her duty to bury her husband?

Menelaus

It is duty's part not to rob the dead of their due.

Theoclymenus

She may go. A wife kept dutiful is to my own
advantage. Go in, and bring the funeral robes of state.
And if you act so as to please her, I shall send
you from my country with no empty hands, to bear
a good report of me; you shall have clothing, not
this ragged state, and food, enough to bring you home
again; for now I see you are in hard case.

And you, my dear, do not wear yourself away in longing
for the impossible. Menelaus has met his fate,
and your dead husband shall not come to life again.

Menelaus

You see your task, young woman; it is to love and serve
the husband you have, and let the other husband go.
In the circumstances, this is the best that you can do.
But if I come through safe to Hellas, I shall put
an end to former scandals that were said of you.
Only be now the wife that you were meant to be.

Helen

It shall be so. My husband shall have no complaint
of me. You will be there, and you will know the truth.
Come in the house, poor wanderer, you shall have your bath

and a change of clothing. Kindnesses I have for you
shall not be put off. If I give all you should have
from me, in all the better spirit you will do
the things my dearest Menelaus has deserved.

(Exit Helen, Menelaus, and Theoclymenus inside the house.)

Chorus

Long ago, the Mountain Mother
of all the gods, on flashing feet,
ran down the wooded clefts
of the hills, crossed stream-waters in spate
and the sea's thunderous surf beat
in wild desire for the lost girl
not to be named, her daughter,
and the cry of her voice keened high to break
through mutter of drums and rattles.
And as the goddess harnessed
wild beasts to draw her chariot
in search of the daughter torn away
from the circling pattern of dance where she
and her maidens moved, storm-footed beside
the mother, Artemis with her bow,
stark eyed, spear-handed Athene
attended. But Zeus, from his high place
in the upper sky shining ordained
a different course to follow.

For when the wandering and the swift
course of the mother was done, the far,
the toilsome, the vain search
for her daughter's treacherous capture,
she crossed the place where the mountain nymphs
keep watch in the snows of Ida,
and there cast the blight of her grief
across the stone and snow of the hill forests.
Earth, green gone from her fields, would give
food no more in the sown lands,

and generations were wasted.
For the flocks she shot out no longer
tender food from the curling leaves.
The cities of men were starving,
the sacrifice to the gods was gone,
no offerings flamed on the altars. She,
turned cruel by grief for her daughter, dried
the springs that gush from deep in the ground,
and there were no jets of bright water.

But now, as those festivals the gods
share with the race of men died out,
Zeus spoke, to soften the ruinous
rages of the Great Mother:
"Go, stately Graces, and go
Muses, to Deio angered
thus for the sake of the maiden.
Change with wild singing the strain of griet
in her, and with choral and dancing."
It was then that the loveliest
of the immortals took the death-
voice of bronze and the skin-strung drums:
Aphrodite. The goddess smiled
and drew into her hands
the deep sounding flute
in delight with its music.

You had no right in this. The flames you lit
in your chambers were without sanction.
You showed, child, no due reverence
for this goddess' sacrifice.
You won the great mother's anger.
The dappled dress in the deer skin
is a great matter, and the ivy wound
green on the sacred hollow reed
has power; so also the shaken,
the high, the whirled course of the wheel

in the air; so also the dances,
the wild hair shaken for Bromius,
the goddess' nightlong vigils.
It is well that by daylight
the moon obscures her.
All your claim was your beauty.

(*Enter Helen from the house.*)

Helen

Friends, all that happened in the house was favorable.
The daughter of Proteus keeps our secret. Though she knows
my husband is here, and though her brother questioned her,
she told him nothing, rather she told him he was dead
and buried, out of the sunlight. She did this for me.
My lord has gained a capture, fair and fortunate.
He took the armor that is to be sunken in the sea
and fitted the shield-handle upon his powerful arm
and wears it so, with the spear held in his right hand,
as if working to help grace the dead man. Yet still
first he practiced, with the armor on him, for a fight
as one who would raise a monument on a whole world
of outlanders once we embark in the oared boat;
then I took off the wreck-stained clothes he wore, and gave
him new, and made him fine again, and bathed his body
at last in fresh water drawn from the stream.
But see,
this prince, who now thinks that he has a marriage with me
in his hands' reach, is coming from the house. Do me
the favor of silence. We want you on our side. Control
your lips, be kind, and some day, if we ever save
ourselves from here, we shall attempt to save you too.

(*Enter Theoclymenus, followed by Menelaus, and leading a group of serving men who carry the funeral properties.*)

Theoclymenus

Men, go on to your work as the stranger told you to
and take with you the funeral offerings to the sea.

Helen, if what I say to you does not seem wrong,
stay here, as I ask you. Your duty to your husband, whether
you go, or stay, will have been done in any case.
I am afraid longing for him will seize you, make
you fling your body down into the tossing sea
stunned with delights remembered from him before. I know
how much, too much, you mourned for him when he was not
here.

Helen

O my new husband, how can I help holding dear
the memory of my first marriage, all the love
and closeness of it? I have loved him well enough
to die when he died. But what grace would he have known
in death from my death? Only let me go, myself
in person, and give his dead body what it deserves.
So may the gods grant you what I would wish to have
them grant you, and this stranger, who is helping here.
For your kindness now to Menelaus and to me
you shall have me in your house, as wife, to the degree
that you deserve, since all this is in fortune's gift.
Now give your orders to the man who will provide
the ship for our conveyance. For my sake do this.

Theoclymenus

Go then, get ready a Sidonian fifty-oar
galley, have master-rowers aboard, give it to her.

Helen

Is not this man to be in charge of the funeral ship?

Theoclymenus

Certainly. My sailors are hereby ordered to obey him.

Helen

Give the order again so they will be quite clear.

Theoclymenus

Again, and still a third time, if you wish me to.

Helen
For your good, and for my good in the things I plan.

Theoclymenus
Now, do not waste yourself with too much weeping.

Helen
No.
Today will show the quality of my love for you.

Theoclymenus
Remember, the dead are nothing. This is wasted work.

Helen
It is matters there of which I speak; and matters here.

Theoclymenus
You will find me as good a man as Menelaus.

Helen
I ask no more. I need only the favoring time.

Theoclymenus
That is in your power, as long as you are kind to me.

Helen
I shall not need teaching to love those I ought to love.

Theoclymenus
Shall I go too and see the expedition along?

Helen
Oh no. My lord, you must not do slave's work for your slaves.

Theoclymenus
Very well. I shall pass the rituals of the Pelopidae.
My house needs no lustration, since it was not here
that Menelaus died. Therefore, one of you go
and tell my vassals to take the wedding images
inside my palace. All my country must be loud
with singing of congratulation and with strains
of marriage for Helen and me, to bless our state.

Go now, my stranger guest, and give all this to the arms
of the sea, in honor of him who was her husband once,
then make haste back to my house again, and bring my wife,
so that you may be my guest at our wedding feast,
and then go home—or stay and prosper here with me.

(*Exit into the house.*)

Menelaus

O Zeus, renowned as father and wise among the gods,
look down upon us. Grant us surcease from our pain,
and as we grate the shoal-rocks of catastrophe
reach us your hand, touch only with your fingertips
and we are there, triumphant, where we wish to be.
Our past has been our share of troubles, all our share.
I have heard, O gods, much said of you. I have heard good,
and hard things also. I do not deserve bad luck
forever, but to walk with upright stride. Grant me
this one grace. It will make me happy all my life.

(*Helen and Menelaus go out at the side.*)

Chorus

Phoenician queen out of Sidon, O
lady of oars swift in the splashing water,
dear mother of oared ships
after whose lead in the dance move
the dolphins, when the open sea
sleeps in stopped winds: may she,
Galaneia, who is called lady of calms,
and the Great Sea's green daughter
so speak: "Set wide the sails on the masts,
leave them free to the salt airs,
but take in your hands the pinewood oars,
mariners, oh mariners,
as you convey Helen home
to kind haven upon the shores of Perseus."
So, Helen, might you find again
the Daughters of the White Horses there by the river,
or before the temple of Pallas

come back at last to the dances
or the revels for Hyacinthus
and the night-long festival
established by Phoebus after
his whirled throw of the discus
in games: for the Laconian land
a day of sacrifices
by ordinance of him, son of Zeus;
come back to the girl you left
in your house, Hermione,
for whose marriage the pine-flares have not shone yet.

Oh, that we might fly in the air
winged high over Libya
where the lines of the migrant
birds, escaping the winter rain,
take their way, following
the authority of their leader's
whistle. And he flying into the rainless, the wheat-burdened flat
places, screams his clear call.
O flying birds with the long throats, who
share the course of the racing clouds,
go to the midmost Pleiades.
Go to Orion of the night,
cry like heralds your message
as you light down on Eurotas,
that Menelaus has taken the town
of Dardanus and will come home.

May you riding down through the bright
air, swift on your horses,
sons of Tyndareus, come
down the stormy courses of your stars' flaring,
oh, dwellers in the sky,
saviors of Helen, come
cross close on the green swell and the dark-skinned back of the
rollers

and the gray splash of the breaking sea,
bringing from Zeus those winds that blow
sweet airs for the mariners:
and cast away from your sister the shame
spoken, of her barbarian loves,
shame that was hers for punishment
out of the quarrel on Ida, though
she never went to the land of Troy,
not to the towers of Phoebus.

(Enter a servant of Theoclymenus, from the sea.)

Servant (shouting)

My lord, the worst of news from our house. We have just learned.

(Enter Theoclymenus from the house.)

Fresh news, strange news and bad. Hear it from me at once.

Theoclymenus

What is it?

Servant

Your work is wasted for a wife who is not
yours. Helen is gone away, out of our land.

Theoclymenus

How gone? On wings, or do her feet still tread the earth?

Servant

Menelaus carried her away. For that was he.
He came himself, and brought the news of his own death.

Theoclymenus

This is disgraceful. But still I cannot quite believe.
What sort of transport carried him away from here?

Servant

Precisely what you gave your guest. He took your men
and left you. There you have it in a single word.

Theoclymenus

How? I must understand this, and I cannot yet
credit it that a single arm could overpower
so many sailors, all those who were sent with you.

Servant

After Zeus' daughter left the palace here, and you,
and was escorted to the sea, there as she placed
her tiny feet, she mourned aloud, most cleverly,
for that husband who was by her side, by no means dead.
Now as we came to your shipyards and your arsenal
we hauled down a Sidonian ship of the first class
with fifty rowing benches to accommodate
the oars. And now our various duties were assigned.
One took his place at the mast, another at the bench,
hands on his oar, another had charge of the white sails,
the steersman sat to the tiller and the steering gear.

Now as we were hard at it, there came down to the shore
certain Greek men who had sailed with Menelaus once
and who had been watching for just this. They wore the rags
of shipwreck. Fine-looking men, but in a filthy state.
The son of Atreus saw them as they came, and made
a false pretense of pity for our benefit,
with: "Poor castaways, what ship? It must once have been
Achaean, cracked up now, and so we see you here.
Will you help bury Atreus' fallen son? His wife,
Tyndareus' daughter, buries him in effigy.
This is she." They then let fall some fictitious tears
and took aboard what was to be sunk in the depths
for Menelaus. We had our suspicious here,
and there were words among us, how these newcomers
were very numerous. Nevertheless we held our peace.
We had orders from you and kept them. You had said
your guest was to have full command. That ruined all.
Now all the cargo was light and easily picked up
and stowed inside the ship, except the bull, who stood

and baulked at going up on the steep slanted plank,
but bellowed aloud, and with arched back and head low down
rolled his eyes round the circle past his lowered horns
forbidding all to touch him. Helen's husband raised
his voice, and cried: "Oh, you who captured Ilium,
come, do it the Greek way, can you not? Hoist the bull's
weight on the strength of your young shoulders, heave him in
over the prow. You, draw your sword and prod him on.
For he shall be our sacrifice to the dead man."
They at his order went and laid hands on the bull
and heaved him up and forced him on the rowing deck,
and Menelaus, rubbing its forehead and its skin,
persuaded him, without harness, to go inside the ship.

At last, when all was got aboard and stowed away,
Helen, with dainty steps, put her feet through the rungs
of the ladder, and took possession of the central bench,
with Menelaus, the supposed dead man, by her side,
and left and right along the bulkheads all took place,
man ranked on man in order (but the Greeks had swords
hidden away beneath their garments).

Then we all
whitened the water at the bosun's shout of "Row!"
Now when we had reached a point where we were not remote
from the land, nor near it either, then our steersman asked:
"Shall we make further out, my friend, or is this far
enough to suit you? What we do is yours to say."
He said: "This will do." Then, with a sword in his right hand,
crept to the prow, and braced himself to strike the bull,
and where he stood, there were no dead men in his mind,
but as he cut the throat he prayed: "Lord of the sea,
Poseidon in the depth, and you, chaste Nereids,
convey me safe to Nauplia's strand, convey my wife
who left it, but was chaste." And as he spoke, the blood
rained on the water, favoring the stranger's prayer.
One of us said then: "There is treacherous sailing here.

We must make back. You, give the order for right oar,
and you, reverse the rudder." But now Atreus' son
stood from the slaughtered ox and hailed his company:
"Oh, flower of all the land of Greece, why longer wait
to smash these savages, cut them down and throw them off
the ship into the water." Then your bosun called
aloud upon your seamen to resist: "Come on!
Get anything to fight with. Take the end of a spar;
break up a bench and use it, or an unshipped oar,
and smash the heads of these foreigners, who turned on us."
Both sides sprang to their feet then. We laid hands upon
whatever ship's lumber we could find. But they had swords.
The ship ran blood; but there was Helen cheering them
on from the stern: "Where is the glory of Troy? Come on,
show it on these barbarians." Then all fought hard,
and some went down, some kept their feet, but a man down
was a man dead. Menelaus had his armor on
and watched where his companions had the worst of it
and there rallied them, with his sword in his right hand,
so that men, to escape, dived overboard. He swept
the rowing benches clean of your mariners, then went
to the rudder and made the helmsman steer the ship for Greece,
and they got the mast up, and a wind came, favoring him.

They are gone from your country. I myself, escaping death,
let myself into the water where the anchor hung,
and as I was failing, one of the fishermen at his lines
pulled me out and set me ashore so I could bring
this message to you. Man's most valuable trait
is a judicious sense of what not to believe.

(*Exit.*)

Chorus

I never would have thought Menelaus could be here
unknown, my lord, to you and us. Yet so it was.

(*As Theoclymenus speaks the next lines, he starts to rush into the house but is met at the door by another servant, an attendant of Theonoë, who struggles to keep him from going in.*)

Theoclymenus

Oh, I have been duped and tricked with women's artful treacheries.
Now my bride has escaped away, and if they could be overhauled
I would make all haste to catch the ship that carries those foreigners.
But at least I can take vengeance on the sister who betrayed
me, who saw Menelaus in my house and did not tell me so.
She shall never again deceive another with her prophecies.

Servant

Hallo, you there, master, where are you going? Is it death you mean?

Theoclymenus

I am going where justice takes me. Out of my way and stand aside.

Servant

It is a monstrous thing to rush to. I will not let go my hold.

Theoclymenus

You, a slave, will overpower your master?

Servant

Yes. I mean you well.

Theoclymenus

No good to me, unless you let me go.

Servant

But that I will not do.

Theoclymenus

Let me kill my hateful sister.

Servant

No, not hateful. Dutiful.

Theoclymenus

She betrayed me.

Servant

It was just betrayal. What she did was right.

Theoclymenus
Giving my bride away to others.

Servant
Others had more right than you.

Theoclymenus
Who has right over what is mine?

Servant
The man her father gave her to.

Theoclymenus
Fortune gave her then to me.

Servant
And fate took her away again.

Theoclymenus
You are not to judge what I do.

Servant
If I am in the right, I must.

Theoclymenus
Then I am no longer ruler, but am ruled.

Servant
For right, not wrong.

Theoclymenus
You desire to die, I think.

Servant
Then kill me, but you shall not kill
your sister while I have the power to stop you. Slaves, if they are true,
find no glory greater than to perish for their masters' sake.

(*As Theoclymenus is about to overpower and stab the servant, the Dioscuri, Castor and Polydeuces, appear above the palace.*)

Castor
Lord of this land, Theoclymenus, hold hard the rage
that carries you off your true course. We are the twins
called Dioscuri, sons of Zeus, whom Leda once
gave birth to, with that Helen who has fled your house.

That marriage over which you rage was not to be,
nor has the daughter of the divine Nereid done
you wrong, Theonoë your sister, but she kept
the righteous orders of my father and the gods.
It had always been ordained that for the present time
she was to be a dweller in your house. But when
Troy was uptorn from its foundations, and she lent
the gods her name for it, this was no more to be,
for now she must be once more married with her own,
and go home, and live with her husband. Therefore, hold
your hand, nor darken your sword with a sister's blood.
Believe it was in thoughtful care that she did this.
We would have saved our sister long ago, since Zeus
had made us into gods and we had power, except
that we were weaker still than destiny, and less
than all the gods, whose will was that these things should be.

This is for you. Henceforward, let my sister hear.
Sail with your husband, sail on. You shall have fair wind.
We, your twin brothers, guardian divinities,
shall ride the open water and bring you safely home.
And when your life turns its last course and makes an end,
you shall be called, with the two sons of Zeus, divine,
have your libations, and with us be entertained
as honored guests by mortals. Zeus has willed it so.
And where the son of Maia first defined your place
when he caught you up from Sparta on the skyward way,
stealing you, so that Paris might not have you, where
the island stretches to guard Acte, shall your name
be known as *Helen*, meaning Captive, for mankind
hereafter; because you were stolen from your house.
For Menelaus, who has wandered much, the gods
have granted a home upon the island of the blest.
For Heaven never hates the noble in the end.
It is for the nameless multitude that life is hard.

(*The Dioscuri disappear.*)

Theoclymenus

O sons of Leda and of Zeus, I will forego
the quarrel I had with you for your sister's sake.
Nor do I wish to kill my sister now. Then let
Helen go home, if so the gods would have it. Know
that you are born of the same blood from which was born
the best and the most faithful sister in the world.
Go then rejoicing for the great and noble heart
in her. There are not many women such as she.

(*Exit. The chorus begin to go off.*)

Chorus

Many are the forms of what is unknown.
Much that the gods achieve is surprise.
What we look for does not come to pass;
God finds a way for what none foresaw.
Such was the end of this story.

INTRODUCTION TO *HELEN*

The Legend

THE variant, according to which Helen never went to Troy, is not found here for the first time. Hesiod, in his lost works, apparently told the story of how it was a phantom-image, and not the Spartan queen herself, who was stolen away by Paris and recovered after a long war by Menelaus and the Achaeans. Better known in antiquity was the work of Stesichorus, the sixth-century West-Greek lyricist and successor to Hesiod. He, it seems, had said certain hard things about Helen, and as a result he lost his sight, which returned only after he had composed his Palinode, or Apology, from which we have his lines

> That story is not true.
> You never went away in the benched ships.
> You never reached the citadel of Troy.

"That story" is, of course, the standard version as told by Homer; the corrected version of Stesichorus, as we learn elsewhere, substituted the phantom for Helen herself.

We do not know where Stesichorus (and Hesiod) said that Helen did go, if not to Troy. We might gather from the lines above that she went nowhere at all. But Herodotus, whose work was published in full not much more than a decade (maybe much less) before our play, had told a different story, which he claimed to have heard from the priests of Hephaestus in Memphis, Egypt. According to these, Paris did steal Helen away, but adverse winds forced him ashore on the Egyptian coast. There Proteus, King of Egypt, was deeply shocked to hear of what was going on; he sent Paris about his business, and confiscated Helen, whom he held in safekeeping until her husband should come to claim her. Meanwhile Menelaus and Agamemnon gathered together a Greek armada, sailed to Troy, and demanded Helen. The Trojans protested that they did not have her, she was in Egypt. The Greeks did not believe this. They besieged the city and finally captured it, only to learn that the Trojans had been telling the truth all the time. Menelaus accordingly went to Egypt, collected Helen, and (after disgracing himself and Greece by an illicit sacrifice involving two Egyptian boys) sailed home (Herodotus 2. 112–20).

Euripides, plainly, has combined these two versions, and perhaps drawn on other earlier writers as well. He uses the phantom-image, but has Helen herself supernaturally transported to Egypt. The image has its Homeric precedent in the image Apollo made of Aeneas, for Achaeans and Trojans to fight over, while Aeneas himself was transported away through the air (*Iliad* 5. 443–53, and compare 21. 595–605); so also, in the *Iliad,* Paris, Agenor, and Aeneas once again were divinely spirited away alive, and set down elsewhere; and so, too, in another play, Euripides himself tells how Iphigenia was caught up and transported away to the very ends of the earth, there to live as a lonely Greek princess among barbarians awaiting delivery by means of a long lost relative whom she herself thought was dead.

Despite these precedents, the play which Euripides presented undoubtedly struck most of his audience with a pleasurable thrill of surprise. Although he used the Herodotean variant, he contrived, through the old idol-story, to remove that stain of dishonor which the Egyptian version had re-attached to Helen. And he exploited fully the factor common to both legends: the tragic futility of that utterly unnecessary Trojan War.

Date and Occasion

Helen was produced in 412 B.C., written therefore during the winter which immediately followed the tragic end (tragic for Athens at least) of the great Sicilian expedition. With that defeat there disappeared, once for all, the strange Athenian dream of conquering the entire west. There remained the war at home, where Sparta now held a strong position. But Sparta had seldom, perhaps never, for all these years been pushing the war against Athens with complete conviction; and perfectly patriotic citizens might well hope, and urge, that the fratricidal war be ended, that Athens should save as much out of the wreck as possible, before things got even worse. It was a year later that Aristophanes, in his greatest and funniest peace-play, made a strapping and genial Spartan wench ably second Athenian Lysistrata in her program to save the Greek world, and *Lysistrata* ends with a lyric in Laconian dialect honoring Helen of Sparta. In his play, Euripides too is conciliatory toward Sparta, not only in his kindly treatment of the Spartan hero and heroine, elsewhere maligned (*Andromache, Trojan Women, Orestes*), and his flattering terms in allusion to Sparta, but also in his sweeping condemnation of war, *all* war, under which the war in hand is necessarily subsumed (ll. 1151–57).

Such may be a part of the political motivation, but the times seem to have generated personal and artistic motives as well. The sordid state of the world between 431 and 403 B.C., which has its effect in tragedies like *Hecuba* and *The Trojan Women*, also drove Euripides to escape from his own conscience with a new type of play, which may best be described as romantic comedy. Using the theme of the lost one found, a variation of the foundling story (employed also in such bitter comedies as *Alcestis* and *Ion*) he indulges himself in an illusion of optimism in *Iphigenia in Tauris* and *Helen*.

The Play

What we have, therefore, is a light, elegant romance written not only deftly but with wit. The dominant theme is paradox, illusion, surprise, all to be summed up in the relation of Helen to that other self, the idol who is not, but in some way is, Helen herself. Triumphantly, the heroine emerges with all the attributes Homer gave her—the charm, the wit, the self-importance and self-pity—above all, the inescapable loveliness (featuring, we guess, a most accomplished actor in a ravishing mask and with a voice that fairly demanded an extra allowance of solo lyrics); but adding to all these, in perfect harmony, the virtues of Penelope. To her, enters her minor Odysseus, Menelaus. The plot saves him from the low character he wore in *Andromache* and is to wear again in *Orestes* and *Iphigenia in Aulis*. No doubt his heroic leg may be pulled a little in the scene where the Portress (a manly woman, typical of Egypt, straight out of Herodotus) faces him down; but Euripides saw the pathos in situations where a great man's strength is worn away by circumstance, in this case sheer fatigue and starvation, and the hero in rags and tatters is so standard a Euripidean figure that we should not suspect farce. Better to take this play neither too seriously nor too lightly. It is romance, but not without recognition of realities, even realities new to tragedy. In *Andromeda*, a part of the same set of plays, Euripides dealt with young love, rarely considered worth bothering about in early Greek literature; in *Helen*, he realizes that there can be real, exciting love between two middle-aged people who are married to each other. Doubtless, all these elements are there in the *Odyssey;* nevertheless, what Euripides gives us here is his own, as he saw and experienced it, in the form of one of his most compact and elegant dramas.